AMERICAN IDOL EXPOSED

JUSTIN BUCKLES
in conversation with Aaron Bale

LuckyBuck Publishing

Copyright © 2011 Justin Buckles & Aaron Bale
All rights reserved.

No part of this book may be used or reproduced in any manner whatsoever without written permission, except in the case of brief quotations embodied in critical articles and reviews. For more information e-mail all inquiries to:
luckybuckpublishing@gmail.com

Cover Design and Interior Layout by Stanley J. Tremblay, www.Find The Axis.com

Many thanks to our friends at VoteForTheWorst.com, be sure to go visit them: http://www.votefortheworst.com

THE STAGE IS SET

August 2008

It was a long day.

That's putting it mildly.

I'd left my home town the day before, enduring the increased paperwork and scrutiny of Homeland Insecurity, the stares and suspicion that come with looking like a soccer hooligan (which by the way is baldest) and then suffering through twenty-seven hours' worth of traveling stuffed into a glorified tin can hurtling through the skies. Actually, the hurtling wasn't so bad. It was the miniature coach-class seats. The Russian gentleman squashed into the one beside me, half in my seat and half in the aisle, insisted on taking the photo of his wife and daughter out of his wallet and kissing it every few minutes in between mumbled prayers to whatever god or dev-il looked after Russian gentlemen hurtling through the skies in glorified tin cans. It didn't help. I had a deadline that insisted I had to not only stay awake for the whole flight, but somehow hope to edit about 150 pages of the latest book. Add to all that the fact that connecting flight—and there's a misnomer if ever there were one—I was supposed to pick up in Chicago O'Hare was grounded due to high winds, turning an eighteen hour journey into a twenty-seven hour one went a long way to convincing me today wasn't going to be my day.

I felt like crap. My skin felt like wax thanks to the pressurized air-conditioning on the plane and the diet of sugar, sugar, and a few carbs to help soak up the sugar.

I was late to the point where the term 'late' didn't really cut it. I was supposed to be meeting my agent and another of his clients in the Roosevelt Hotel in the heart of Hollywood for breakfast. I have to admit, I'm a big fan of the American breakfast, and the hotel does a very nice fresh fruit pancake. It's as good a way as any to start the day. Anyway, breakfast was going to become evening meal thanks to the Gods of Travel.

Everything was, to put it bluntly, peachy.

Thankfully, there was coffee. Lots and lots of coffee. Coffee is my oldest friend. Coffee never lets me down, forgets about a date we were supposed to have or jilts me for one of the cooler kids. We go way back, me and coffee.

It wasn't my first visit to LA, but again, as the plane banked over the endless lights of the city I was struck by just how vast the place was. The lights just go on and on and on from horizon to horizon. It's hardly surprising people go there—filled with the hopes and dreams of the Bright Lights—every day only for the place to swallow them whole. It's a sobering sight. You certainly don't get to forget your place in the overall scheme of things.

Anyway, when I finally debarked the second plane in LAX I would have made a great extra in the next Romero zombie movie. I followed the other shuffling people toward the baggage carousel. Of course my suitcase wasn't there. That would have been too easy. So the next hour was spent trying to track it down. Turns out it was still in Chicago and would be joining me the next day, so I went out, hailed myself a cab and settled in for what should have been the forty-odd minute drive to the hotel.

Of course it wasn't going to be that simple. There are days you just know the world is having a laugh and you're the butt of its warped sense of humor. The freeway ramp we needed was closed for filming. Special effects crews had been crashing a helicopter into it for the last few hours, or so the taxi driver explained. So forty minutes became seventy, but being the talkative soul that I am, I was treated to quite a few 'celebrity stories' by the driver. That's another reason I love LA, it's not just surreal, we're talking layers of surrealism upon layers of surrealism.

It had been a few years since I'd stayed at the Roosevelt on Hollywood Boulevard. It's a wonderful old-style hotel right in the heart of Tinsel Town. Across the street is the Mann Chinese Theater, Sid Graumans famous movie hall, dwarfed now by the elephants of the Kodak Center. The red carpet was out for some premier or other, as were the costumed super heroes. There were a couple of Darth Vader's, Spiderman (in a very grubby Spidey suit), Marilyn Monroe, Goofy, the Dark Knight. Only in Hollywood... I smiled, tipped the driver and headed to the check-in. The last time I was here there had been an air of fading grandeur about the hotel but I'd absolutely loved the place. This time I walked through the door into something best described as brothel-chic. It was dark. I mean dark. I could barely see a few feet in front of my face. Of course I was coming in out of the light so they could see me just fine. My agent, a big burly guy with hound-dog cheeks came barreling up and pumped my hand.

"Aaron, Aaron, good to see you, my man. There's someone I want you to meet. Aaron, meet Justin Buckles. Justin, this is Aaron Bale." He pronounced it wrong, bay *all* instead of bay *ull*. I've grown used to people mangling my name so I didn't correct him.

An unassuming guy with a buzz-cut, dressed in Levi's, a T-shirt and a pair of Puma's pushed himself up out of one of the leather bucket seats and came forward to shake hands. "You boys need to talk. What are you drinking?"

I didn't know whether it was midnight or midday, and was tempted to go for another coffee but figured he was buying so what the hell? This is one of the few perks of being a writer, a publisher's lunch we call it, so I opted for a nice 12 year old Macallan single malt, no ice. It's my drink of choice when I actually drink, which isn't often. Of course, the agent returned with one iced tea and one iced coffee. I grinned, toasted the guys with, "Hell, I'm a writer, Hemingway gave us something to live up to," and settled down in my chair.

We started talking about everything and nothing.

Justin had flown in from Portland to get together with the Writers Guild to prep for his wage claim hearing. I was the second bird to be killed with one stone. He told me how he'd spent the last decade working behind the scenes on just about every show imaginable, and was a mine of gossip, stories and scandal that I could have listened to for hours if I hadn't been dead on my feet.

Of course my agent had an ulterior motive for setting up the meeting. Justin had stories he wanted the world to know and he figured I was the guy to help Justin tell them. It was a job interview.

It took less than fifteen minutes for me to find myself agreeing with him. It wasn't my usual remit, I'd ghostwritten books for various celebs and interesting projects like that under various names, and I'd just finished a ghostwriting project, but this was different. It took me out of the realm of the familiar. And, I confess, I'd always fancied myself as a bit of an investigative journalist. That's my way of saying they had me at hello. I just listened. That's one thing I like to think I am good at. But it was obvious after maybe an hour nursing the scotch, my mind boggling at some of the stuff I was hearing, that Justin had more stories than I could possibly take in in the few hours before jet-lag owned my soul, so we made plans to meet up at the coffee shop across the street the next day for breakfast and more stories.

"I've got a feeling this could be the beginning of a beautiful friendship," I said as we parted, me for my room and some well-earned sleep, Justin to prepare for his wage claim hearing. It was a Hollywood line, but we were in Hollywood, so what else was I supposed to say?

* * *

From here on in, 'I' is going to refer to Justin. Aaron Bale ceases to exist.

These are his stories, in his words.

The names have not been changed to protect the innocent, the guilty, or anyone else for that matter.

Let's completely ignore Julie Andrews' Do-Re-Mi advice from The Sound of Music and start at the end. I've always been more of an X,Y,Z man than an A,B,C one. Trust me, in this case, it's a very good place to start...

VERBAL ABUSE

It wasn't anything new to be told that I was "fucking worthless" or that I was "a complete fuck up." It happened on a weekly—or if I was really lucky daily—basis.

Verbal abuse in the office was as commonplace as sitting fender to fender in the snarl of traffic that was rush hour L.A., but this time was different, because this time it was my family that were being attacked.

Let me summarize the wisdom of my boss, Wylleen May: my parents did a horrible job raising me, they were shit, not just shit but complete pieces of shit actually, they would never amount to anything (despite, logically approaching retirement and had amounted just fine, thank you very much,) and should be embarrassed by the fuck-up of son that they raised.

The thing is for most of my time on the show I'd simply blown this shit off because it was part and parcel of the place. It happened with such frequency, and not just to me, but to a majority of employees, that they almost seemed right. How frightening is that?

This time she crossed the line.

The attack was meant to hurt me. It wasn't about putting me in my place and making me a good little worker-drone.

My father's health was failing fast. He had been exposed to Agent Orange, as well as various tainted vaccines while serving in Vietnam. It's not a story unique to him but that didn't make it any easier for the people who loved him. Being the kind of person I am, with my parents living in Oregon and me working in Los Angeles, I felt as though I should keep my boss up to date on my father's health. It was pragmatic if nothing else. I wasn't looking for sympathy. The fact of the matter was one phone call and I could be on the next plane. My father had been diagnosed with Hepatitis C, Lymphoma, Diabetes, severe Anemia, two blood disorders and severe liver damage.

My boss knew this.

She knew everything about my father's health.

Here's the thing, even though I didn't think that much of her as a human being—I mean there's a limit to how many times someone can call you a fuck-up and fucking worthless and maintain your respect—it was tough. Sometimes I just needed to unwind, sit down and talk to someone about what was happening. And, as odd as it sounds, part of me still thought of her as a surrogate mother figure. I thought I could confide in her. I thought I could talk to her about stuff, including my father's failing health.

If you ask me, my parents did a pretty amazing job raising me.

I was brought up knowing right from wrong. They instilled me with morals and values from an early age. I was taught the value of money, and, of course, I was taught to believe that you should treat people the way that you wanted to be treated.

I had given my two week notice the Friday before the verbal onslaught. My boss was very pleased that I would be moving on. Pleased for me. She encouraged me to take the other job I had been offered because it was a way for me to expand my knowledge of the entertainment industry. The following

Monday we were taping the Green Mile show in Pasadena. As soon as taping wrapped for the day, I was called into the production office.

As I entered the room I was told to close the door behind me and take a seat. She said it in that tone. I did what I was told, but before my backside had made contact with the chair, the tirade began. It was a torrent. Words spewed out of her mouth. Frothed. And they just kept coming. I was worthless. My parents were pieces of shit. I would never amount to anything. People would laugh in my face at the new job. I didn't have the skills to perform properly there. Without her, without this place, I was nothing.

It didn't take a rocket scientist to tell me this barrage of abuse wasn't because I'd done poorly at my job, far from it, the fact of the matter was I'd been a great employee, I'd performed amazingly well on the job and she was losing me to another production company. She was, for want of a better term, pissed off that I had grown bored (amongst other things) where I was and wanted to move on.

Let's talk professionalism: if I had done a lousy job and she was attacking me because of it, why bring my parents into it? The focus would have stayed on me, and on the things I had done wrong. That wasn't how it went. She yelled, she screamed, she ranted, but not once did she say I'd done something wrong in the workplace. She was out to hurt me. Let's put it bluntly, she wanted to punish me for leaving her. She was acting like the jilted lover. It was spiteful. She knew how ill my father was. She knew that he was dying a slow, tortuous death.

And what did she do?

She threw it in my face.

I knew that my father's life was being cut ridiculously

short. She knew that was something I had been struggling to come to terms with. That's what makes her abuse so much worse, if you ask me. I knew my father and I weren't going to have much longer together, and I had all of a son's guilts and wants and grief.

In fact, he passed away just over two years later, having been diagnosed with close to two dozen separate illnesses and diseases, as well as three forms of cancer, all of which could be traced back to his war-time exposure to Agent Orange.

During Wylleen's onslaught I didn't say a thing. Not one word. I just looked at her the way I always did when she unleashed her 'Tourette's' tongue. Of course, she didn't actually have the excuse that a sufferer would have, just the ability to turn the air blue.

At the end, when the words had started to choke in her throat because she was gasping for air and trying to shriek at the same time, she collected herself enough to inform me that I was no longer welcome in the office, and only had the next few minutes to reconcile my petty cash, company credit card receipts, and all of those other duties that went along with my job title as Idol's production coordinator.

This meant I would be in a position to start the new job sooner, which was great, actually, because I would be being paid the proper wage for the job title, close to double what I was making with Idol.

Despite the absolutely inexcusable nature of it, it was fairly comical watching her go off on a tear, gasping for air, face turning puce, multiple chins wobbling every which way but loose as she struggled to find a new way to call me a loser.

I had to bite my tongue in order to stop myself from laughing at one point. I'd become so inured to her bullshit laughter was pretty much the only medicine. But laughing at her now was only going to escalate this shit, and, to be blunt, given her color, the veins popping out of her temples and pounding at her throat, and her inability to breathe and yell at the same time, I was more than a little worried she'd clutch her miserable (and metaphorically withered) tit and keel over. The last thing I wanted was her death on my conscience.

So instead, when she'd run out of steam, I simply said, "Are you done?"

IT SHOULD HAVE BEEN RAINING

It was all very ritualistic.

I packed up my laptop, put my walkie-talkie back on the charger (making sure to sign it in as I had signed it out. I didn't want to be billed its replacement value for want of a signature on the right piece of paper,) grabbed my backpack and headed down to the car. I made damned sure to tell every single person that I ran into exactly what happened. I couldn't leave without tracking down the production assistant and letting him know the proverbial sword of Damocles was hanging over his head now—or rather the nickel of Damocles anyway. I could well imagine my boss and the production manager flipping a coin in the office to see who'd have the pleasure of canning his ass—and that he would be wise to start looking for another job.

As it goes, he was fired just two weeks later. It seems that's how long it takes in Hollywood for the penny (or in this case nickel) to drop.

Back at the office, I blasted through all the paperwork that I needed to do so that I could get the hell out of Dodge. One of my final acts before making like a shepherd and getting the flock out of there was to write a memo to the accountant informing him that I'd bought a dozen or so pizzas for everyone on the crew using my person credit card because all of the show's petty cash had gone for the beer that filled the numerous production coolers, and asking for a full refund to be mailed along with my final paycheck. I stuffed everything into an envelope and slid it under his door.

Finishing the ritual, I grabbed a banker's box and loaded up everything that was on my desk, as well as, I confess, several items that weren't mine; a couple of reams of copy paper, a slew of office supplies, pens, paperclips, that sort of thing, and a framed picture of one of show's employees who passed away, some empty binders, and a couple of t-shirts. Knowing it would only shrivel up and die in that shit-hole like everything else did, I took the plant that sat on the corner of my desk. The last thing to go in the box was a dollar bill that someone had written "Lucky Buck" on. It had been pinned to my bulletin board.

I still have it in my wallet today.

But for all that, I'm not going to lie to you and pretend I was some Shane riding off into the sunset, or Destry riding again. I was sad. It was the end of a chapter in my life. Life's weird. Normally when it's happening to us we can't see the chapter breaks, save for the obvious ones, the deaths and the divorces. But when I walked out of that office I knew I was writing 'End Scene' on that part of my life. I almost imagined I could hear the clapperboard coming down and the director of my life saying, "Good job everyone, that's a wrap."

Don't get me wrong, it wasn't some sort of existential angst. It wasn't because I was suddenly unemployed, or that I wasn't going to be part of the *American Idol* scene, but more because the show, the abuse, the exploitation, the drugs, the alcohol, and everything else that I had dealt with during my time on Idol had molded me into the person I was. And sometimes a bit of reflection, perspective, and self-awareness is a good thing. I knew what was happening, what I didn't know was that it would take the best part of three years to write it down. But the simple act of writing it now is cathartic.

In the movie of my life it would have been raining, but it never rains in Tinsel Town and a backdrop of smog and forest fires just isn't as romantic, but then you very rarely see the truth when you're dealing with the thief of dreams...

MANUFACTURED REALITY – MY FIRST DAY

It's not what you know, that's the old adage, right? Well, I guess there's a little truth of that in every walk of life, and therefore in every story worth telling.

I got the job on *American Idol* through a friend whose mother worked as the show's music supervisor. I had worked with her on a couple of projects, including a short film, and didn't feel bad about asking her to pass my resumé along to her mom in the hopes that she, in turn, would pass it along to the person in charge of hiring and firing, the show's production manager.

It was all about timing.

The Season 2 auditions were approaching, and they were due to be held at the Rose Bowl in Pasadena.

Of course, for all the leg-ups in the world, you still need to be able to cut it when it comes to the crunch. If you can't, it doesn't matter who gave your resumé to whom.

I was hired to work as a production assistant for a few days during the open auditions in Los Angeles. I had to be at the Rose Bowl at roughly five in the morning. It was my first day being thrown under the bus. In other words, Situation Normal All Fucked Up as another Band of Brothers liked to say.

As I pulled in, and followed the signs, all I could see were people. It's hard to explain the absolutely incredible sight that is one great mass of people waiting for their shot at the dream. Even though the sun was far from fully up, hope had taken on a distinctively sweaty, human, smell. People were singing and acting out, hoping to be seen before they were supposed to be seen, as though it would give them a leg up. Not that you could see anyone's 'Star Quality' for the sheer overwhelming press of bodies on all sides. It was all just one big writhing mass of wannabe superstars. I'm sure they could make a horror movie out of it if they set their minds to it.

And, of course, everything was already behind schedule. This, I quickly came to realize, was standard operating procedure. Or, in other words, schedules were made, optimistically, to be broken. Before the floodgates opened up for the tidal wave of humanity—the first audition—one of the senior producer's, David Goffin, called an impromptu meeting of the production assistants. This, too, was standard operating procedure, the sloping shoulder of blame redistribution. We all gathered about, waiting for the inevitable. He was seriously pissed off and made no bones about it and no effort to hide it. It was all our fault. That was the message semaphored by his curt gesticulations and snide words. Of course, I called it the sloping shoulder of blame, because the fact that everything was running behind was down to Goffin and his tier of management. They were the ones charged with keeping things on schedule.

One of my first conversations—or perhaps we should call it a light-bulb moments—involved being told it was fucking bullshit that the production assistants caught all the flack when it was obvious the headless chickens running about pretending effectivity while being incapable of organizing the proverbial piss up in a brewery were the root cause.

I did a theatrical eye-roll at the suggestion that this was all my fault.

My first day and I was already being thrown under the bus, but at least there were dozens of others doing the swan dive with me. There were two ways it could go from here, I could shrug, do the day's work and be done, or could bust my hump for the day and hope there was still the potential turn this gig into a long term job.

So, my hump got busted.

In truth, the day was just like any other day, average, uninteresting, save for one little piece of theater I thought was brilliant: the producers were walking up and down the line, hyping up the crowd, feeding them with lines to say and when to scream and shout and jump up and down, all delivered via a megaphone.

This was a reality show...

All be it a manufactured reality that bore no resemblance to the real world whatsoever. But that didn't matter. What mattered was what the public would see on their television screens. It was all smoke and mirrors, like the best illusions and the cleverest confidence tricks.

SMOKE AND MIRRORS

The events at the Rose Bowl wrapped up and things were moved to the Renaissance Hotel in Hollywood for the Los Angeles call-back round.

The first day of call-backs was held with the executive producers of the show, Nigel Lythgoe and Ken Warwick, in situ.

I must have made some sort of impression the day before, because I was put in charge of running the room, which meant making sure there were always contestants on standby, that they knew the audition rules, and the mundane stuff like where to stand when they entered the room to sing for Nigel and Ken.

Yeah, to sing for Nigel and Ken.

Not the judges.

I didn't think anything of it at the time, but once the shows started to air I felt like Dorothy pulling back the curtain and seeing the little bearded man back there pulling the levers. The majority of the auditions you see on the air are the ones that take place for Nigel and Ken, not the actual judges. It's all carefully orchestrated. The entire set up for both is exactly the same. The same dance floor, same background, just different rooms and judges. Smoke and mirrors, or more accurately, the magic of television. In the final edit the illusion is polished and the watching world is led to believe that everyone auditioning gets the opportunity to stand up and sing in front of Randy, Paula and Simon, but the truth is that out of the several thousands of hopefuls that turn up in each city less than 400 actually do.

BOY'S TALK

Another part of my job that day was to check in with Nigel and Ken regularly to make sure they didn't want to take breaks. This meant I got to interact with them a lot, even if only to be sure they didn't need anything.

Whenever I did I was treated to 'boy's talk'. You know the sort of thing: how unbelievably hot some of the female contestants were, great racks, luscious asses, and of course, making fun of the less fortunate ones. You see, good TV isn't about the best voices or the tightest asses, sometimes it's about mocking the poor bastards who've lined up for hours and hours for the privilege of being mocked. You know the ones. You've seen them on TV. And I suspect you've grasped the fact that they were only allowed to get that far in the audition process specifically because the show needed people to make fun of when it aired.

I'm no saint, don't get me wrong. I'm not going to pretend I didn't join in, thinking it was fun at first, but that's the thing, at first I wanted to fit in, to find the same things funny that the rest of the did and be part of the crew. Mob-mentality. It was all about ingratiating myself with the douchebags. The shine wore off soon enough when the reality of just how badly they were exploiting these kids for laughs and, of course, the all-important ratings, sunk in.

This was the first time I saw Mike Darnell and Tom Sheets, both executives at Fox, and way too important to say a word—even hello—to anyone who did not have the requisite 'executive' in front of their job title.

GOOFY

Okay, confession time: I was star struck the first time I saw Simon, Paula, and Randy. I was. I admit it.

First impressions.

Simon: Short, hairy, and reeked of stale cigarettes.

Paula: Jesus where do I start? Okay, here's the overriding first impression that sticks with me when I think about it: it was as though she was at prom and had just been crowned queen. She was all smiles, waving at the contestants and their parents as she strolled through the hallway into the judges holding room. And, like every good Prom Queen on her big night, she was just a little wobbly.

Randy: Black sumo wrestler.

I can't say that I was similarly star struck by Ryan, but then he had been present during the Rose Bowl auditions. It was, however, obvious that the success of the show, coupled with the fact that he was the sole host at this point, had gone straight to his head. Putting it bluntly, he just wasn't that pleasant to be around. Kind of like "Hey I am in the room now, everyone stop what they're doing and stare." He was also a little on the short side, maybe shorter than me, and I am only 5'8".

The final judging days arrived for the Los Angeles auditions, and I again was put in charge of the area outside the judging room. The mood was very heavy this time around as the contestants who had made it through the round with Nigel and Ken were now sweating bullets and nervous wrecks. As far as they were concerned, this was it, make or break. When they walked through the door they'd be performing for the judges. My duties were the same; brief the contestants on what to expect; tell them to find and stand on the x on the floor; and, of course, wish them good luck.

One auditionee stands out so vividly even now, because the guy was so incredibly nervous because he had a secret. If the judges happened to ask him what he did for a living he couldn't tell them. Sounds ominous doesn't it? But he wasn't Harry Reems or any other undercover porn star come to strut his stuff. He wasn't a mass murderer for that matter. He was, get this, Goofy. Yep, Goofy as in the Disneyland Goofy that kids queue up to get their photos taken with in the Magic Kingdom. Apparently it's all hush-hush top secret pain of death stuff. According to him, his contract expressly said he wasn't ever to reveal that he was a character. He was more scared of the potential consequences of blabbing his secret identity on national TV than he was of the actual audition. Now of course had he been Spiderman...

PAULA AND COREY CLARKE

Shortly after the auditions were over and done with, Hollywood Week took place in Glendale.

Funny thing about the street lights in Glendale: the design embossed on the bases of the old street lights have swastikas on them. That sticks out in my mind. Another thing from back then that sticks out in my mind is the Paula and Corey Clarke sex scandal that began right around that time.

I remember it like it was yesterday. It was all so Hollywood: him walking from the stage to the judges table, grabbing Paula and serenading her while they swayed back and forth. Her gazing into his eyes.

It was odd.

We all thought it was odd.

Looking back with the 20-20 of hindsight I have no doubt that most (if not all) of it actually happened.

Of course, that is just my opinion. I wasn't a fly on the wall. I wasn't some voyeuristic little perv peeking out of any closets or in the room next door listening to the bedposts banging against wafer thin walls.

I can remember the layout of the theater, and how the contestants all hung out around by the front doors (the same area where the judges would arrive and depart for the day) so it's not beyond the realm of possibility that someone from

Paula's team could have slipped Corey her phone number at that time, or in Nashville, as he states after he made it through to the final round of auditions.

Phone records did conclusively prove that he did have her number, and that they spoke on numerous occasions over the months that followed, and Trenyce from Season 2 went on record that Corey was regularly gone from the mansion, which she found very odd.

I didn't think much of his "performance" for her at the time, or the fact that they might as well have been dry-humping on the judge's platform. People will do pretty much anything for a shot at 'fame', but the shit would have to hit the fan eventually. Shit has a habit of doing just that.

When the story finally broke, the show was on the road.

We were St. Louis holding the auditions for Season 4.

All hell broke loose that morning. The hotel we were staying in was under siege. I felt like Steven Seagal. The Press were everywhere. They scented the kind of grist that kept the mill going round and around and around. The hounds of hell were at the door and the security team was in full-on panic mode. Panic, of course, was a natural state of affairs as far as security was concerned. Perhaps it was because the head of security was more interested in getting head than running the company? Who knows, but that's a story for another day.

The initial buzz amongst the guys on the ground was focused on the likelihood that the deed had almost certainly been done. Smoke and fire, right?

Paula was in her hotel room. She needed to be told. No one wanted her to find out by hearing it on the news or reading it in the paper. My understanding of what went down that morning goes something like this: Paula was briefed about what was going on in her hotel room, then ended up doing the walk of shame to the production office with the help of security and her entourage. What I can say for sure is that she was in tears because I saw her exit the elevator, the giant sunglasses doing nothing to hide the tears. That, and of course, the hand full of tissues she clutched was a dead giveaway.

The public relations reps for the show were in tow. They were ever-presents traveling around the country with us from audition to audition, their cellphones surgically attached to their ears.

I wasn't sure if it was a joke or not, but word quickly spread throughout the crew that we were to gather all of the newspapers in the place, and that included all of the papers the hotel had delivered to the occupied rooms, as well as going on a scavenger mission through the seating areas of the hotel, and throwing them in the trash because the gossip pages included a nice juicy story about the sex scandal. I didn't take it seriously, of course, I mean, who would? So I didn't bother to trash a single paper. I was hungry so I went and ate breakfast instead. We were told to avoid Paula and not to make any eye contact with her, which, let's be honest, wasn't much of a hardship. I was already doing that.

I am not a big fan of crazy.

Several months after we returned from the audition tour, the interview with Corey Clarke aired on television. The execs at Fox and the show's producers were not looking forward to it, but I'm not going to lie, the rest of us were. In fact we were looking forward to it so much the show bought food in. We set up theater-style seating in the back office, had beer and wine, and watched the interview unfold, while the producers were in their offices, wailing and gnashing their teeth and just wanting it to be over with damage limited, the fall out contained. It was pretty obvious we were all thinking the same thing by the time the interview was over. As witnesses go, he was pretty damned credible, and for the most part we believed him. Show producers can say over and over that Paula was the den mother and gave her phone number out to all the contestants. It's the party line. They've said it until they were blue in the face, but I worked on the show for several seasons and don't ever once recall this happening.

In fact, on reflection, if it did happen surely it would lead to friction, wouldn't it? It smacked of favoritism. As employees we weren't supposed to interact with contestants – we signed a stack of paperwork agreeing to that – why would it be fine for the judges to?

So, if you ask me, the den mother excuse is bullshit; it's sole purpose to avoid further embarrassment.

Add to that the fact that since the scandal broke a number of contestants from various seasons have come forward, on the record, to call bs on the notion of Paula being the den mother, exchanging numbers, and speaking with them on a regular basis.

Contrary to the party line, they said that they had zero interaction with any of the judges.

Put it this way, I know who I believe.

CONTROVERSY AND COCAINE

Hollywood Week wrapped for Season 2 and the stand out, without question, was Frenchie.

Absolutely amazing.

We were all blown away by her.

Of course, she was removed from the show for showing some skin, a wonderfully hypocritical move to generate some controversy. There was no other reason for it. There's a double standard that runs right through the core of *American Idol*. It wasn't like Frenchie was the first, or the last, to show a little skin. Hell, she wasn't even the worst, but the others were allowed to stay while she was booted. Here's the thing: it isn't about fairness, it's about buzz; it's about controversy. The show needs people talking about it, which means it needs its quota of controversial moments to fill each season.

Frenchie was just one of those: a controversial moment.

It's just a damned shame, because no one on Season 2 came close to her talent-wise.

On the last night of Hollywood Week I was offered my first bump of cocaine by another employee.

I respectfully declined.

WORDS OF WARNING

I was very impressed with myself: I was a part of one of the biggest shows on television, I had moved from Coos Bay, Oregon (a beautiful small coastal town) to Los Angeles without a plan, without a job, and without much more than the determination to work in Hollywood. In a way, I felt like I had it all, the whole enchilada, though the reality of it was my employment on Idol was little more than a couple days at that point and there was no job offer on the table.

But I still felt like I had made it enough to start bragging.

I had a few family members, cousins actually, that lived in the Pasadena area and regularly had dinner parties and real big blow-out family BBQ's at their houses. One of these took place shortly after Hollywood Week for Season 2 wrapped, so one of those poor, huddled masses, I headed over for the free meal and the leftovers that I knew my cousin would make sure I had as I headed home afterwards.

My cousin's godfather has worked in Hollywood for several years, from the Hollywood Bowl to the CMT Awards in Vegas, and once he got wind that I had worked on the show he pulled me aside to give me the *"I've been around the block, this industry's in my blood, you're the fresh meat, so listen to what I have to say"* talk, which I had no choice but to listen to because he towered me. There I was, backed up against the wall, while he asked all about Idol, making small talk before diving in head first and throwing up red flags about the show left, right and center.

He told me in no uncertain terms that he wouldn't want to work on the show (the image his words burned into my mind was of hell being decidedly frosty and monkey's dancing in front of a cracked and broken tombstone) because he had friends who had, and they'd been treated like shit. Some of it was money. They had a reputation for not paying correctly, he said, so I needed to stay on top of that and make sure my paychecks tallied.

It was all good stuff.

But the single most profound moment of wisdom he imparted was about my soon to be boss.

He told me that he had experiences with her - the kind of experiences that quickly helped him make his mind up that he would never work with her. Not all of the stories were bad though. Some were worse. He told me that she waddled like a goose because she was the size of a Volkswagen Bug, looked like and had the nickname Jabba The Hut, you know, the crime lord from Star Wars. He also said that the reason she wore so much perfume was because, due to her obesity, she was physically unable to keep herself clean in all the areas that liked to reek. So, in order to cover the wafting eau de natural she bathed in perfume before she left the house. Literally. Later on this little tidbit was confirmed by one of my co-workers who was in the restroom with her and threw up into her mouth due to the absolute stench that came from the stall next to her.

While I took the words of my cousin's godfather to heart, I figured the old guy was a natural storyteller and that he was just making things bigger so they sounded funnier.

Exaggeration is the key to good humor. I figured he was gearing up for some big joke at my expense, you know, family stuff. Welcoming me to the madhouse. The alternative was he was just another pissed off former employee with an ax to grind. I didn't for a minute think what he was telling me was the truth, the whole truth and nothing but the truth, so help him, God.

I listened though, and I remembered everything he said.

I wasn't so far down the road when I realized that every word he said was gospel.

JOAN RIVER'S BREATH MINTS

I hadn't heard from anyone at Idol for a while so I figured that I wasn't one of the chosen few taken on full-time after Hollywood Week.

I went job hunting.

It didn't take long to land work at E! Entertainment as a production assistant. I wound up working in the art department for the 2004 Awards Season and got to attend (because I was responsible for assisting in the setup of the E! interview and commentary areas on the red carpet and back stage,) just about all of the award shows that year.

The most memorable meeting/moment during these couple of months was Joan Rivers.

She was genuinely very nice, and very high maintenance, and she had the scariest face I have ever seen. Literally.

The first time I saw her rehearsing for the red carpet, I had no idea who she was. It was from a distance, I admit, but I couldn't make out who she was meant to be. Once her mouth opened, I did the mental math and put two and two together: the burn victim/space alien I'd been staring at for a good 20 minutes was actually Joan Rivers.

Her dressing room was always stocked with Listerine strips, and I freely admit I helped myself to handfuls every time I had the opportunity. A boy has to stay minty fresh in Tinsel Town, after all.

AMERICAN JUNIORS

My E! Entertainment job was wrapping up when I got the call.

It was my friend (the same friend who had been instrumental in fixing me up with the Idol gig through her music supervisor mother, remember her?) She had been hired as the head production assistant for a new show called *American Juniors* that would be starting production out of the Idol office while Season 2 was still on the air. She offered me a production assistant position, and I bit her hand off, well figuratively at least. It meant at least six months of full time employment, which meant six months of rent, six months of food and gas and living. It meant a little bit of security. In Hollywood security is a rare and precious thing.

I had no idea what the job would entail, but quickly got a handle on my duties.

It wasn't long after I was hired that the majority of the producers and the head production assistant left Los Angeles to travel around holding the nationwide auditions. My main job was to process all the paperwork that was being shipped back by them on a daily basis. The majority of the paperwork was made up of personal releases, which were needed for everyone that appeared on camera. As the auditions progressed and the contestants were confirmed for the final round of auditions in Los Angeles, I had to contact each family and let them know that they would need to be filling out releases for each and every family member, and I mean every family member, no matter how extended and tenuous their link to the family was.

The main purpose of these releases was to get them to state, in writing, that their lips were sealed. There'd be no speaking to the press about their loved one's involvement with the show. It didn't matter if it was Great-Grandma who had just turned 100 or the newborn infant that was only a month old. Loose lips cost lives... erm... jobs, at any rate. The show might thrive on controversy, but every controversy had to be managed, manufactured. I'm not kidding, there wasn't a single day that went by where I wasn't asked if I was serious, and I'd explain I was just doing my job. One mom literally thought this was joke as she had several kids and a newborn and she needed to fill out the paperwork on behalf of each of them, even though one couldn't talk yet and the others had no idea what was even going on, let alone what talking to the press entailed. It was all a bit silly.

I was also asked on two separate occasions if I was Justin Guarani from *American Idol* Season 1. I said yes and told them that the show felt sorry for me because I came in second place so they decided to supply me with a job until I could get my music career up and running. What can I say? Sometimes sitting behind a desk is mind-numbingly dull and you have to take the crumbs of amusement when they're offered, right?

The only thing that really bothered me about working on the show was the fact that the producers lived for the contestants crying. There's something wrong with humanity when the pièce de résistance of a 60 minute show is some poor kid breaking down in tears.

And they were.

There were contestants crying in every corner and against every wall, as the thief of dreams claimed theirs, and the producers were loving it. Whenever a contestant cried, a camera was shoved in their face, or the face of their mother or father or whoever was there to look after them because the only thing better than tears was a great sound bite.

It's all about the drama, the theater, the so-called reality. It's just not a reality that any decent human being would want to live in.

WYLLEEN THE HUT

It's hard to describe my first interaction with Wylleen as interaction because interaction assumes active participation on both sides.

It went something like this: I was with the head production assistant. She knocked on Wylleen's door and waited for permission to enter. Inside the hallowed office, we sat on the couch. Her office was full of empty birdcages and horse memorabilia. I couldn't help but wonder if there was some subconscious symbolism going on with the empty cages. This was, after all, the woman my cousin's godfather had warned me about.

It didn't take a lot of imagination to work out where the Jabba The Hut nickname came from. There was certainly a family resemblance. I was introduced as the new production assistant for *Juniors* and that was that. See, this is what I mean about interaction assuming active participation on both sides. Jabba didn't say a word. She basically sized me up like a rack of lamb she might have been interested in gobbling down, you know the sort, the eyes roll from the feet to the midriff to the face and back down to the feet. I did my best to be cordial whilst worrying if I were about to wind up on the dessert menu, and said, "Nice to meet you."

It was uncomfortable.

Actually, it was a nice glimpse into the show from the side of the contestants. I felt as though I was being judged on everything from my Pumas to the bulge in my Levi's and how I filled out, or didn't, my t-shirt. The line from the old Smiths song stuck in my head, about how meat is murder. I certainly felt as though I were auditioning for the role as meat.

I wasn't asked a single question.

That was it, over as quickly as it had begun.

Because Idol was being produced out of the same office I had plenty of interaction with the producers, some of whom remembered me from the Season 2 auditions. Of course the question came up as to why I wasn't hired to work in the office for the season? Ours isn't to reason why and all of that.

It was refreshing to be able to hang out with the couple of production assistants that I had grown close to while working on the Idol auditions.

Okay, confession time: I've always been the kind of guy that listens into and eavesdrops on conversations I'm not supposed to be listening to. What can I say? I am curious soul. Aren't we all? It's natural to want to know what's going on, what's being said about who, what's the dirt being dished. We want the skinny, the low-down. What we don't want to be is the only one in the room who doesn't know what's what.

I started to give in to my natural curiosity more and more as the Clay/Ruben drama kicked off.

I was in the heart of the Clay/Ruben sing-off each week.

It was abundantly clear that Clay was the standout artist, and frontrunner to win the season. And what was equally clear was that it bothered the people on the inside. Eavesdropping was regularly rewarded by catching derogatory comments like "fag" and "fatty" being thrown around the office. It wasn't subtle, not that subtlety would have excused it. And who were the worst offenders? You guessed it, the producers who were busy putting the shows together and writing the storylines (what, you didn't imagine reality wasn't scripted did you?). They'd deny it, of course, but who else would the producers be referring to? The topic of conversation was always the show, and Clay had just graced the stage in that matching red pants and jacket outfit.

Clay's sexuality was up for discussion on a daily basis. It didn't help matters that he never removed his make-up after the show was over. His sexuality wasn't just the topic of office gossip, either. It was being discussed everywhere from the tabloid television shows to the news rags and gossip magazines that fed on this kind of stuff.

Everyone who worked on the show knew he was gay.

I am sure the producers were concerned about the implications of what would happen if he ended up winning the season. Hand on heart, I honestly believe that.

And this is the sadness of something made for public consumption: the people in the office were terrified Clay winning would alienate most of America. I heard from more than one person that the Big Wigs dreaded the possibility of Clay going public with his sexuality because it would turn off too many viewers, and in turn those precious record sales would plummet. The bottom line was it was all about the bottom line. They dreaded the possibility that the show wouldn't stay the money making machine it had turned into.

You don't need me to tell you how wrong that particularly Neanderthal notion is, we've all seen the way America has embraced Clay, and you don't need me to tell you just how high he has risen. Ruben? Well it's as if he never existed.

SIMON LYTHGOE AND KIMBERLEY LOCKE

Before *American Juniors* had wrapped up, I was offered a job on the Season 3 of Idol.

I started right before they headed out on the road for the Season 3 auditions.

This season for me started with the Simon Lythgoe/Kimberley Locke sex scandal. There was idle talk (get it? Okay no more bad puns, I promise,) and plenty of juicy rumors suggesting that they had been dating for a while. Although no one could confirm when it started, there was speculation that it started during the show when the contestants were staying in the mansion.

It was procedure for the producers to stay at the mansion with contestants, one male, one female, just to be present in case anything were to happen, to keep an eye on things and make sure no problems surfaced. Twenty-four hour security was in place, too. This arrangement continued well after the show moved the contestants into apartments closer to the studio.

The logic, I think, of the arrangement went one step further than simply looking out for the contestant's needs. The producers were trying to sell a behind the scenes Real World type of reality show using footage from back stage, the mansion, photo shoots, etc. The sight of Season 2's producers clutching handheld cameras wherever they went was a common one. They would do quick interviews after photo shoots in the hopes of getting candid reactions to 'surprise' events that happened, document the weekly clothes shopping for the performance, etc. From what I heard editors were working on putting together a couple rough episodes of this new Behind the Scenes show that they were going to pitch to networks.

The idea had potential, the show was a massive success at this point, and we've already established that the world loves a good gossip, a little salacious titillation and glimpsing those unguarded moments when people let their hair down. It's the entire basis for reality TV. While the material was being scoured for the best sound bites, the juiciest footage, film of Kimberley Locke brushing her teeth in the bathroom showed up. The gentleman alongside her filming was Simon.

The talk around the office was that they were getting hot and heavy. She was wearing a robe, he was dressed.

When all this was unfolding something puzzled me, and it didn't stop puzzling me if I am honest about it. Everyone has to sign a release stating that they will not have any form of relationship or physical contact with the contestants during the season and up to six-to-twelve months after the last show has aired.

Kimberley's response to this, although one of those great political dodges of neither admitting nor denying, states that any relationship she had with anyone involved with the series started after the competition ended.

But let's not beat about the bush here, there's absolutely no question they were in a relationship. She used to show up with him on set all the time. She was constantly around the set during the beginning of Season 3. I don't remember her being around for very long, but she was definitely there. She would show up and follow Simon around like a little puppy dog, and when she couldn't follow him she put on her nice face, transparent as it was, and chatted away painfully with other staff members until he returned.

Of course there were plenty of other scandals, many very much office based, that came out after Season 2 ended, one of my favorites being the STD that miraculously passed from contestant to contestant. Oh yes, that didn't make the papers did it?

I'll make no bones about what really pissed me off (and a fair few other employees) about the Simon/Kimberley relationship wasn't that he was 'getting some' or anything juvenile like that. It was that he was almost certainly violating the agreement that we'd had to sign, but nepotism would protect him. Violation or not, nothing would happen to him. He was the executive producer's son and if the shit hit the fan had his dad to cover his ass. So what did a signature on a piece of paper matter?

COCAINE AND TIMECARDS

On my first day working on Season 3 I was offered coke.

And not the cola variety.

Cocaine was so abundant we might as well have been working in the fields of Cocaine County, Columbia, and not an office in Hollywood. That said, I'm not convinced the executives had a clue of what was going on under everyone else's noses.

I watched it being cut on desks. I watched employees head out to their cars for a quick bump or two for lunch. I listened to employees joking about how coke was what got them through the fifteen-hour shifts stuck inside the editing bays reviewing the footage and putting the shows together.

Since I was no longer on *American Juniors*, being dedicated 100% to Idol meant I was right in the mix as a production assistant. My duties could be pretty much summed up thus: whatever needed done, if I was around, that was my job. That ranged from washing towels, to picking up lunch for the contestants, running errands, taking contestants to and from wherever they were staying, and just about everything in between. Production assistants are typically the slaves of the show, second class citizens, disposable people. That was certainly the case on Idol. The production assistants were the grease that kept the show running smoothly and picked up all the slack.

Day by new day I realized I was being taken advantage of.

I was working my ass off. For too much of Season 3 my working week was seven fifteen-plus-hours-a-day days. My reward was roughly $110 a day, or $550 a week, regardless of whether it was a five or seven day week. After taxes and such I was bringing home five to six bucks an hour. Barely, and I mean barely, enough to survive in Los Angeles. I was living in Sherman Oaks, just over the hill from Beverly Hills, a typical two plus hour round trip drive through that horrendous Los Angeles snarl laughably called traffic. My typical dinner consisted of a few slices of bread, maybe a peanut butter and jelly sandwich if I had the energy to make it, and not much else.

I make no bones about it: I was poor, dirt poor, even though I was working as much as eighty hours a week.

Not that it mattered a damn to anyone. What we should and shouldn't write on our time cards was a running argument. Believe me, I tried time and time again to write my actual hours down and submit it to the accountant at the end of the week. And nine point nine times out of ten I might have gotten away with slipping the real numbers through and been paid for the work I had done, but for the most part, all the time cards I tried the honest approach with were returned by either the accountant or the shows production manager.

The problem with my cards seemed to be the fact they were accurate when really what they wanted were generic times for each day of work, regardless of how many days I had worked in any given week. And it wasn't just me. We were all in the same boat. I argued my case the first few times this happened because it was a matter of principle. I should have been paid for each and every second I was on the job. We all should. If you have a punch in punch out system you get paid for the hours clocked up and the work done, it isn't like having a salaried position where you pull in X per month regardless of the hours worked.

I got the distinct impression some of the higher ups were taken aback by the fact that I stood up for myself. That didn't help me much. After going through the same rigmarole time and again, I threw in the towel and went along with what the show wanted me to do. Suddenly my time cards all started at exactly the same time. I would "clock-in" at seven am, and "clock-out" at eight pm, making sure to throw in a one hour lunch from one 'til two or two 'til three just to mix it up. That became the 'reality' of my working day. It didn't matter when I worked, what days I worked, or how long I worked. They wanted generic time cards with at least twelve hours worked with a full hour written in for lunch. The irony is I never, and I repeat never, got a full hour for lunch.

The rationalization we were given was that production days, be it in television or movies, were recognized as a twelve hour work days by the State of California and they were not required to pay you for anything more than twelve hours unless they had a particular urge to do so. Like I said, I argued with this several times, but it wasn't like I was Sisyphus with that damned stone to roll up hill, I was more like the Wicker Man building the pyre under my own ass. Every time I argued, I pissed someone else off.

So I made my own rationalizations: the show was a massive success, the more friends I had on the inside, the better I did my job the more chance there was of turning this into a multi-season gig.

Like I said, I was living the high life, I had it all. Apart from a decent meal and sleep, you know, basic stuff like that.

MORE DRUGS

The head production assistant for Season 3 had worked the Season 2 auditions with me and then been picked up to work in the office for the season itself. I can vaguely remember working with him during the auditions, but nothing really stands out from those few days. It was all a bit of a blur. He was a tall guy, coming in at well over six foot, and, putting it politely, dumber than a bag of nails. Logic suggests he was hired because, like Superman, he could lift incredibly heavy things, alas he couldn't leap tall buildings in a single bound and he wasn't faster than a speeding train, but you couldn't have everything. He had this nervous twitch. When he wasn't twitching, he was talking. When he was talking, if it wasn't all about the war, it was some nutso conspiracy theory or other. He was, to be blunt, a very peculiar guy.

Of course that crackpot nuttiness could well have been fueled by the stupendous Adderall addiction the guy had. Adderall, for those of you who aren't up on your psychostimulant meds is nasty little combo of amphetamine and dextroamphetamine. Supposedly it works by increasing the amount of dopamine and norepinephrine in the brain to increase alertness, sex drive, concentration and transform you into a Duracell bunny of creativity. I guess he'd taken Morpheus' advice to heart and taken the blue pill, and the red pill for good measure, and kept on taking them like they were tic tacs.

There were two production mangers, but the reality of their situation was more like one was a senior production manager and the other his assistant. One of them, the one who didn't act like a production manager was a year older than I was. Shorter, stocky, and hairy. I want to say he had a rather equine face, but that's far too diplomatic. He looked like a horse. For the most part, he was a cool guy. You know the type, the run of the mill frat boy schooled in Santa Barbara and possessing a singularity of purpose that included pussy, the bald man in the boat, the bean, the ax wound, the bearded oyster, the bearded clam, beef curtains, beaver, bush, poontang and any other creative spin on the word vagina that could be found. He was a regular pornaholic.

I'd say once every couple of days I'd see some sort of porn pop up in my inbox courtesy of him. We got on just fine. Most of our conversations revolved around sex, you know the sort of guy talk that devolves to a running list of who we'd had, who we hadn't, who we would given half the chance, who we'd sell our left nut to, and how we would go about the doing in graphic detail. That's the frat boy mentality. I went along with it. Here's the thing, peer pressure isn't something you stop caring about or stops pressuring you even when you go out into the real world. Remember what I said about long term planning and dreaming of a multi-season contract? That meant staying on the good side of the right people. And the right people were the people further up the food chain. So I played the game. I talked the talk.

His partner in crime was this bleached blonde smiler. She was always happy. I mean unusually happy, we're talking painfully happy. She was very, very good at her job. She was forever picking up the slack left dangling by her frat boy partner. She was a typical southern California blonde, loved Nordstrom and lived for gossip. Products lined her desk: for her face, for her dry elbows, for the puffy skin beneath her eyes, to reduce her age and fill in wrinkles before there were wrinkles to fill in, and other creams for various body parts, and the necessary assortment of perfumes for every mood and possible occasion. There were framed pictures, too. Not loved ones or children. Framed pictures of *herself*. There was another one hanging on the wall behind her.

Reading back through these last few paragraphs it sounds like I didn't like them. I did. I'll admit it. I liked both of them.

But...

You knew there was a 'but' coming, right? Most of what I did for them and with them during our time together on the show was all about saving face and getting on their good sides. I had a plan, and that plan was all about securing my job for the season, and if I was lucky a few seasons down the road. I am not an idiot. I know how to play the game. I know who I need to be friends with when it comes to getting ahead.

PARTNERS IN CRIME

My true partner-in-crime was another production assistant who worked the Season 2 auditions with me. We were on very similar wavelengths, could talk shit with the world's greatest bullshitters, and just generally bonded in the perversity of the job. We worked well together, which was useful because we had to work side-by-side for the best part of every day. And, like me, she knew most of what passed for office politics was bullshit. It helped to have someone there to vent to, and I think me being there gave her an outlet for her frustration. And we were frustrated. Frustrated and exhausted most of the time.

The cocaine I was constantly offered started to look better and better. People around me were corroding their nostrils because they were truly being worked to the bone. My sleep patterns were shot. I was genuinely exhausted, I mean bone-tired, but every time that coke was waved under my nose I declined.

HOLLYWOOD WEEK

Everything kicked into high gear when the guys returned road weary from the Season 3 auditions. Hollywood Week was careening toward us like an out of control truck. I had done the Hollywood Week for Season 2, as well as *Juniors*, so I had a fairly good idea of what I was getting myself into, how it was all going to unfold, and pretty much everything in between.

I was on-call during Hollywood Week, same remit as ever, if someone needed something, anything, I was to rush over and take care of it yesterday. But this time, as an added bonus I was placed with a producer to help log and record the paper trail, write down what they were doing, when, who they were interviewing and what was being said. It was only for a couple of days during the week. Good paperwork left everyone stain resistant. Hollywood Week's a frantic time for the contestants. Most of them spent the days in a state of permanent panic born from not knowing what to do, where to go and more often than not, who they were. It was a three ring circus of blind clowns and acrobats without a cane between them.

From day one I'd had my suspicions that the show was rigged. Too much was at stake for it not to be. It was hard to believe the reality they were selling was even remotely close to the real thing, especially after the whole Clay/Ruben fiasco.

Hindsight is always 20-20, and opinions are like assholes, you know, everyone's got one, but between you, me and the gatepost I'm not exactly going out on a limb in saying Clay was the standout and should have won the season. So, suspicions deeply rooted, I was always looking for things that seemed out of place, things that didn't fit. It was like the old kids song: *one of these things doesn't belong, one of these things is wrong.* I was constantly on the lookout for that one thing that would justify my deep-seated doubts about the validity of the show. Remember, it was claimed over and over that Idol was a true reality show. Nothing was manufactured.

The first thing that set my spider senses tingling was the producer's behavior during Hollywood Week, especially the one I was placed with. She seemed to work very hard to instigate the slightest drama between contestants during her interviews with them. Camera crews were everywhere, covering every angle. And thanks to the magic of the editing suite, that footage could be spun into some really good television.

It was like one of those horror movies where the monster is always just lurking at the back, in the darkness, waiting to pick the weak ones off first. Any signs of weakness or distress during the interviews was pure gold as far as she was concerned because she could create some drama for the cameras. What could possibly make better TV than a bit of mental anguish? She had a fairly standard template of questions that ranged from, "So, how to do you feel about so and so and their performance?" to "Do you think that such and such out sung you on stage."

She was always picking away, trying to get them to bite and come back with something that would make their fifteen minutes of fame that little bit more memorable. What she didn't do was ask personal questions, it wasn't about how they felt they did on stage, how they performed, how they coped with their nerves. It was all about the other contestants. Of course, with all the contestants wanting to be bigger and badder than the last one, their comments were invariably snarky, just a little bit bitchy, and could easily be manipulated in the final edit to offer some of that carefully manufactured drama where in truth there was none.

I can vividly recall the producer going back and forth between female contestants amping things up by dropping carefully crafted lines like, "I heard that there's some drama going on between you and so and so. What happened between you two? I thought you were friends?" You know the sort of thing, designed to elicit a response along the lines of, "Well fuck that bitch, she can kiss my shiny metal ass."

They were the perfect sound bites, especially because any swearing could be bleeped out and the show's logo slapped over their mouths when the filth started spewing.

VARIOUS TYPES OF HELL

There are various types of hell. There's the hot fiery hell of damnation. There's the icy hell of blizzards and snow and cold that no one on earth can bear. And then there's Hollywood Week with its fifteen-to-twenty hour workdays that has everyone run ragged. Our job was to arrive first and leave last. The whole time card debacle and not getting the wages we'd earned should have already made it fairly obvious the show didn't follow the standard twelve-hour turnaround time for employees. The truth of the matter is it was very rare for me to get a twelve-hour turn around. And we're not just talking Hollywood Week. We're talking right across my entire time with the show.

Without the uppers, downers, pick-me-ups and drop-me-offs, that veritable pharmacopeia of prescription and illegal narcotics to help me do the walk of life, I was a zombie. It wasn't uncommon for me to crash at my desk at around three or four. Luckily, I don't snore.

Hollywood Week shifts went into the wee hours of the morning. You'd usually be able to find the contestants rehearsing with Michael Orland and Byrd, the vocal coaches, for the group songs well after midnight. Given the day usually began around 7am the toll would quickly begin to tell on moods and humor. We were staying until two or three in the morning, driving home only to arrive with barely enough time to shit, shower, and shave before we had to turn around and be back on site bright-eyed and bushy-tailed just a couple of hours later.

Down in the trenches we all bitched and complained about it. The truth of the matter was all of the production assistants were led on when it came to working hours and commitments to the office and Hollywood Week. When I signed on and given my paperwork for Season 3 I was told that I would be working twelve-hour days, never more, because the show didn't allow it and because we were only paid for twelve-hour shifts. But, if we were called on to work more than twelve hours we'd be compensated for the extra time. Never on the one hand, compensated on the other, hmm a contradiction. It's like saying usually never, it just doesn't add up. Never is an absolute. A twelve hour day is the standard Hollywood work day, fifteen hours, twenty hours, isn't. So do you blame me for feeling that I'd been lied to and taken in because I was young enough and naïve enough and stupidly willing to work my ass into the ground because it was my dream to work in TV? I was a sucker. I fell for it.

But there's only so much shit you can shovel before you start talking back, asking questions, and eventually pissing people off when you call them on their broken promises and do something stupid like demand to be paid for hours you've put in.

I put in close to one hundred hours during Hollywood Week.

I was paid for sixty of them.

Psychiatric Evaluations

The contestants who made it through to the final group had to go through psychiatric evaluations and speak with counselors before they were able to head home for the week. This typically took place in the hotel where they were housed. It was my job to shuttle them to the airport after the evaluations were complete.

We weren't supposed to interact with the talent, but who's going to sit in a car for an hour and say nothing? So, being the opportunist that I am, I took it upon myself to get the conversation going, ask how they were doing, how they were enjoying things, and work my way around to the chats with the counselors. The good thing about the contestants is that they had no censor button so they were quite happy to chat away about everything, spill whatever went on behind closed doors and share how they really felt about things. Generally they just enjoyed a bullshit session when they had the chance.

During Season 3, I spent a lot of time around the contestants and for the ones that were under eighteen, their guardians.

So, the typical drive-to-the-airport conversations were something like this: "How was the week? I bet you're exhausted?" Stuff that passed for small talk in the rarified air of the dream factory. I'd slowly worked my way into the, "So how'd you get on with the counselor?" line of not quite so small talk.

There were always a few contestants in the van, so once the ball got rolling they started sharing their stories and talking amongst themselves. They told me they were asked if they ever thought about setting people on fire, if they ever thought about suicide or heard voices, if they had demented thoughts or suffered panic attacks, if they took medication for anything, and on, and on. Basically they were trying to figure out if these kids were going to melt down and harm themselves or harm others. Admit to fantasies about burning the next-door neighbor while hyperventilating in a brown paper bag and trying to drown out the devil's voice yammering away inside their skulls and they were out.

Joking aside, it made sense to be asking questions, no matter how odd they might seem. No one knows how they're going to cope with the spotlight of fame, nor the artificial intensity of being thrust into it and suddenly becoming this commodity, this thing that was worth so much money to so many people. If things went tits up the finger of blame was going to point squarely at the show. In a blame culture nobody wants to be culpable.

Of course that didn't stop some of the contestants feeling violated – their word not mine – but violation's part and parcel of the fame game. If you don't like it, if you don't like the idea of paparazzo pointing their intrusive lenses into your face while you're in Walmart or Duane Reed, if you don't crave the napkins being thrust in your face in restaurants when you want a 'quiet meal with a loved one', if you don't want them tailing your car or chasing you or hounding you off the beach because their telephoto lenses are hungry for a nipple slip they can sell for good hard cash, then don't sign up to be a part of it. It's as simple as that. Nobody's holding a gun to your head. Nobody is forcing you to sing for your supper. It's your choice. It's your dream.

At Idol they're just packaging it for you.

I INHALED

After Hollywood Week wrapped for Season 3, I took the first toke of my Idol employment. I shared a joint with a producer and couple production assistants in the parking lot at CBS (where the show's offices were located and the show was shot). We puffed away in broad daylight, in the middle of the lot, security cameras watching our every move. CBS security guards were just a few feet away manning the fort for the day.

I inhaled.

I did.

But do you know what the best part of it was? Not the company. Not the smoke. Not the venue.

I didn't have to pay for it.

RANDOM DRUG TESTING

One year ended and another one began, Father Time's scythe slicing into 2005. Coming back from the holidays I expected some sort of not-so-random drug and alcohol tests to take place. It's not like we were athletes ramping up for the Olympics, but it was the beginning of a brand new season and workplace D&A tests are relatively commonplace in Hollywood. You expect it. It goes with the territory.

That said, I was never tested on *Juniors* but I assumed that was because they had already been done before I joined the crew. Talking like this makes it sound as though I was a big drug guy. I wasn't. And the depth of my innocence stretched to the fact that I knew I had smoked that joint a few weeks before and I had no idea how long it took for traces of any illegal substance to flush out of my system. A day? A week? A month?

Over the Christmas vacation I made a point of drinking plenty of fluids, figuring I'd help my system flush out any "weed". I've got no idea if it helped, but it kept me regular. I really didn't want to be pink-slipped for a couple puffs on a joint.

I panicked. I looked online for all the ways I could cleanse my body (imagine someone going through my browser history and seeing drugs, detoxification and other choice words in the cache!) and anything else that I could do to get the toxins out of my system. If I had known any Native Americans, I'm sure I would have badgered them into taking me along to a sweat.

In the end something approaching rationality took hold.

I hadn't smoked pot in several months before those CBS parking lot puffs so I figured the odds of anything lingering this long in my system were slim to nonexistent. Of course, after making myself physically sick with worry over the drug testing, nothing happened. There were no drug screens. Not then, not later. Not during any of my time on the show.

I guess they didn't want to have to fire 80% of the crew.

There was no alcohol testing either.

The only tests I remember were ones of endurance and patience, basically tolerance tests like 'how much bullshit you were will to take before you snapped?'

In other words no credible testing for anything that actually mattered. They certainly didn't do any background checks on the production assistants. No driving records were pulled even though the production assistants were responsible for chauffeuring the contestants around. To say it was off is an understatement in the same way as saying Tiger has a weakness for 'strange' is.

In fact, no one was ever really interviewed for a production assistant position. The process went something like this: candidates were called on the phone and asked if they were available to work. If they were, they were told where and when to show up. If they turned up, they got the job, no questions asked. But, of course, it wasn't like they were handling secrets of national importance or anything.

I guess that's why so many of the shows employees took

advantage of the fact that they could drive around Los Angeles stoned.

You doubt me? Hand me a bible and I'll happily swear on it that I, for one, did this time and time again. I'd smoke a joint or take a few hits out of the pipe that was forever being passed around the parking lot. Who needs a joint when you can take a bong into the CBS parking lot, eh? It is not like security were going to bust us, and we weren't going to turn ourselves in. So, for a while there I was smoking pot every day, on the job. I never hid it. None of us did. We were out in the parking lot toking away. The producers would walk by and say "hi," and act as though seeing us getting stoned was the most natural thing in the world to encounter in a television station parking lot. That, or they'd linger to take a hit themselves.

The joints weren't confined to the CBS lot, either. I remember smoking at the contestant's mansion. What I'm saying in my not too subtle way is that drugs were a massive part of the show. And they were still a massive part of the show when I left, so it doesn't strain credulity too much to imagine that they still are.

Personally, I never did anything more 'stonerish' than smoke pot during Season 3. I can't say the same for others though. Cocaine was the big one, and as we rolled into Season 4, pills gained popularity amongst the crew. Pill canisters were carried around in pockets just like car keys.

Look, I'm not an idiot, I know how incredibly fucking stupid it was to be stoned behind the wheel of a car. Forget the fact that I was responsible for the lives of fifteen other passengers in the van as I sped through the curvy roads of the Hollywood Hills, high as the proverbial kite, but no one stopped me. No one gave a shit. They'll say they had no idea what was going on, but that's just ass-covering. Just like the CBS parking lot security guards, they looked the other way.

YOU'LL JUST HAVE TO HOLD IT

By the time Season 3 kicked off, the basic routine was set in stone.

I was put in charge of credentials which was a fancy way of saying that I had to compile a list for each show that consisted of staff members, Fox employees, Fremantle employees, and any guests that would be attending for the day.

We had multi-colored wristbands that I was responsible for handing out during the morning and early afternoon on show days. The actual colors varied because, like everything else to do with the show, no one could ever make up their mind what they wanted. The colors represented how much access the wearer would have to the staging area and office area. Regular staff members always received full access, while most of the Fox and Fremantle employees had limited access, and guests had the least of amount of access possible. More often than not Wylleen preferred that guests didn't get a wristband at all. She wanted them to stand in line to watch the show like the rest of the ticket holders, and she had final approval of the guest list. This meant that every show day I'd have to waste time tracking her down to ask her permission regarding who got what access. Add to that the fact that I'd receive emails from all the executives at Fox and Fremantle pretty much around the clock asking me to add this person or remove that person, or beg me for special access for a certain someone else, and you'll appreciate that it was a headache.

Sometimes that damned list could keep me glued to my computer screen for the entire two day block that the show aired.

Toward late afternoon (after distributing all the wristbands to the regular employees) I had to set up a table in the parking lot so that the Fox and Fremantle employees, and any guests, could grab their wristband from me before heading inside to the studio. Each and every time this little arrangement became a fucking fiasco and left me drained and miserable. Picture this: I was outside with the blazing California sun blistering my pasty white skin. We aren't talking about an hour or two here, it was always five or six hours at a time.

My first day out there I terrified I'd screw up so I sat there broiling in my own sweat whilst trying to do my best as I dehydrated and waited for the show to officially start so I could pack up my things and get the hell out of the sun.

I can still remember the weird way the ground swayed beneath my feet as I ran in to the office in search of water. I dumped my shit on my desk. I staggered over to the kitchen and gulped down glass after glass after glass of ice cold water until I almost made myself puke from my need to drink. The second day was different, wiser to the hell I was about to go through, I grabbed a few water bottles and took them with me. Forewarned is forearmed, right? I was certainly more relaxed this time around. So much so I felt comfortable taking a swig of water now and then. And knowing just how long I was going to be out in the sun I loaded up on water before heading out to set up my table.

You know where this is going…

I hadn't been handing the wristbands out and checking

people off the list for more than twenty minutes when I felt the pressure building on my bladder and that need to piss just kept on building and building inside. Thirty minutes and all I could think about was taking a leak. An hour and I couldn't think at all. And still that obsessive need just grew and grew until I swear I thought it was going to rupture and come leaking down my legs. That's the amount of discomfort I was in. But the line was huge. It snaked all the way across the lot and out of sight, and every one of the people in that line was waiting for me to validate their credentials and give them their precious wristbands.

Of course, and this is typical for Idol, no one else could hand out the wristbands. That was 'my' job, and even if someone else could, I was close to half way across the parking lot so it wasn't like I could just wave someone down and ask them to spell me. But needs must as the Devil drives and all that. I called the head production assistant on the walkie-talkie and asked him to send someone to relieve me so I could relieve myself. I could visualize his shrug as he told me no one was available and I was just going to have to hold it.

The clock ticked on and the pain in my bladder just intensified until it became excruciating. And of course I couldn't think about anything else, which only served to make it worse. In my head I was John Hurt strapped down to the operating table in Alien. My entire belly felt as though something was alive in there and ripe to burst out, look around the CBS lot, and go for the person at the head of the line. Which, as far as I was concerned, would serve them right for not letting me take a piss.

Sweat peppered my brow. I couldn't sit still, not that I could stand either. I couldn't find a position that would take any of the pressure off, and frankly I was desperate to do the only thing that I could by then. I had no choice. I let some of it leak out, just a little dribble, but it was blessed relief. I'm not proud of it, and thinking about it now is humiliating. It was all I could do to hold back on the urine tsunami that wanted to wash away the entire parking lot. I didn't give a reason to the guy at the front of the line, I just pushed myself up and ran as fast humanly fucking possible. Usain Bolt would have been left trailing in my urine wake as I ran by the CBS security booth and dived into the men's restroom near the judges dressing rooms. I barely made it, and I mean barely. It was the best non-orgasm I've ever had, we're talking far, far more intense. It was just so good to get it out it isn't funny. And the aftermath, that heady rush that followed the steaming stream of piss, was better than any drug high, believe me. It was euphoric. Who would have thought the removal of bladder pain could be so good? I took one giant sigh, zipped up, and walked out of the restroom.

I headed back to my vacant desk. Of course word had gotten back to Wylleen that I had abandoned my station, and plenty of people were pissed off that they had been forced to stand in line waiting. But better to be pissed off than pissed on, I reckon.

NO BREAKS FOR THE WEARY

"BUCKS" the shout came blasting over the walkie-talkie and right into my ear courtesy of the headsets we wore during show days. Bucks. That was my nickname.

"Yes," I answered back.

"Where the fuck are you? Why aren't you at your table?" Jabba howled back.

What was I supposed to say? I didn't want to give the Fox execs a freebie golden shower? I was cheap, but I wasn't that cheap. In the end I just told her the truth, when you have to go, you have to go.

"No one could relieve me and I had to use the restroom."

"I don't fucking care. Just get back to your desk!"

Thinking about it, this was probably the first time she really laid into me with that foul mouth of hers. Still high from the post-piss euphoric rush, I blew it off and returned to my job. It wasn't until later that I realized that what really irked me about the whole dressing down was the fact that everyone who had a walkie-talkie on had heard her yell at me for taking a piss. The entire crew was wired for sound, and just about everyone was tuned to walkie-channel one.

A couple of hours later the show went live so I wrapped up and headed upstairs. When I got up to the office it was deserted, which was par for the course. Most of the crew were downstairs watching the show from backstage, or from the staging area outside the soundstage.

When the show wrapped everyone returned upstairs, including Wylleen. She threw me the kind of look that could have frozen a penguin in an ice floe, then left me for ten minutes to stew before she summoned me into her office. I went in and was met by a very curt "sit" and a fat finger pointing to the chair beside her desk. Never in my life had someone yelled so ferociously or foully at me. We're talking blow-drier treatment. I just sat there taking it. She yelled herself apoplectic. One of her choicer gems was to tell me that when I was at the table outside, pissing myself was preferable to abandoning my post. That was the official line. It didn't matter how desperate I was, I wasn't to use the restroom. I'm surprised she didn't want to water board me as a punishment for having the temerity to urinate. She kept insisting I'd picked the job, and the only thing I was to think about during show days was doing the job.

It was patently absurd.

Hell, it verged on physical abuse. Granted, no one was hitting me or beating me, but come on, not being able to go to the toilet is barbaric. We're talking extreme and needless distress and discomfort, and as far as I'm concerned that makes it a form of physical abuse. It was like something devised for the Inquisition.

The idea of being fired for taking a piss was so ludicrous I almost couldn't believe it was even a possibility. But I wasn't the only one forbidden from visiting the porcelain god. One of the receptionist's was chastised on numerous occasions because the executives were afraid that they would miss a call if she wasn't at her desk one hundred percent of the time. It isn't like people could hold the line, or here's a revolutionary idea, leave a message...

THE DISNEY BITCH

One standout memory from my time as 'credentials coordinator' was the Disney Bitch. That was my pet name for her, and before you say it, no I'm not talking about Billy Ray's daughter, Miley. It was getting on for mid-season and, as ever, I had a line that stretched out into infinity in front of me. The line had grown from my first few weeks in the lot thanks to the fact that I was now holding the standby tickets and making sure the recipients of the golden tickets arrived safely, got their precious tickets into the Chocolate Factory, and made it into their seats. I had help with the first part of it from the travel coordinator who mercifully dealt with all the shows travel, accommodations, seating, car services, and ticket arrangements so I wasn't supposed to do all of that stuff as well.

During one of those hotter than hell Southern California days, already irritated by the heat, the dehydration and the urge to piss that always seemed to rear its ugly little head when I was in the lot, this woman approached the table. There was no waiting her turn. She cut through the line and walked right up to me like she had every right in the world to. There are plenty of people like that in Hollywood. They all think their time is worth so much more than everyone else's and to hell with common courtesy or good manners. They are, of course, idiots. Unfortunately, that only serves to allow them to act like even bigger idiots.

Watching her sashay toward me I knew it was going to be one of those moments I lived for... not the good moments that left me feeling all warm and fuzzy inside (those were reserved for the urinal after hours out in the blistering sun), the bad ones that invariably left me with a miserable hangover without the joy of having gotten drunk first.

"I am with Disney," she said by way of introduction. Short, sharp and to the point. Close up, she looked ragged. Her glasses were crooked and she had I just got nailed, hard, hair. "I'm here to meet with Simon."

"Fabulous. Do you have a name?" I responded.

She gave me her name, and being the smart-ass I absolutely can be when the mood strikes, I took my sweet time flipping through the credential list hemming and hawing as my finger moved down the names in slow motion. I knew every name on the list. I'd been staring at it all day. She wasn't on it. I pursed my lips and extended my vocabulary adding "okay" and "yeah" to the "Hmmm" but I didn't actually say a word to her. I'd been out there a long time. I didn't care who she was, who she was seeing, or why she thought she was important enough to just breeze by everyone else and come to the front of the queue. Stuff like that just pissed me off.

"What's the hold up?' She yipped at me like an aggressive little pooch.

I shrugged my best I-couldn't-give-a-fuck shrug and told her, "Your name's not on the list so I can't give you access. Sorry." Then over her shoulder, "Next."

"My name has to be on the list. Simon's expecting me. He knows I am coming for an interview. I'm meeting him in his dressing room." She said, clearly frustrated.

"No." I said back. The simplest word in the world to say, and the most frustrating one when it's coming from a lowly production assistant's mouth to deny you the access you need. It's a conversation ender.

"You need to call someone down here, now." She snapped.

"No. You need to step aside so I can get on with my job. You've held me up enough already, cutting in front of everyone when you've got no right to be here," I said, as calm as you like. She pulled out her cellphone and started frantically jabbing away at the tiny keys.

I put her out of my mind and set about helping everyone else in line, who were no trouble at all (maybe they were worried I wouldn't let them in) while she yipped and yapped away on her phone. Every now and then I caught some not-so-muttered complaints about yours truly. After maybe five minutes she shoved her phone in my face and said, "They want to talk to you."

I gave it a moment then offered another who-gives-a-fuck shrug and said, "No thanks."

I didn't care who was on the phone. Rules were rules, and I could be a real jobsworth if I felt like it. She wasn't on my list. The list had a deadline of twelve noon on show days. If you didn't get your information to me by twelve sharp then you were shit out of luck. I'm not going to lie, the job had it perks, and one of them was that I was able to slam the door in the faces of a lot of Hollywood players who thought they were God's gift to the rest of us mere mortals.

The look on her face was, as Mastercard likes to say, priceless. "What do you mean you don't want to talk to them?"

"I mean I don't want to talk to them. The list's been finalized since twelve, your name's not on it so there's nothing I can do. The rules are the rules. No exceptions. You're just gonna have to try again next week."

"Simon is waiting for me," she said, her voice spiraling now into that slightly shrill range that presages a giant industry shit-fit. Suddenly, I wanted to just say the one thing that would tip her over the edge.

"Simon's not even here," I said, lying through my teeth. "He doesn't get here until right before the show starts." It was a safeish lie. People were generally very good at letting me know when Simon had guests, which wasn't often.

"How about this, get Simon on the phone and have him tell me," I suggested. It almost sounded like I was being helpful.

"I need to speak to your boss now!"

I got on the walkie-talkie and radioed for Wylleen. She was the person who said yay or nay to everyone. I told her, in front of everyone in line, including the Disney Bitch, "I've got a very angry woman here saying she's with Disney and that she has a meeting with Simon in his dressing room... Um hum...Yep. She's not anywhere on the list. Not this week, not last week's or any previous ones that I can see." Wylleen's response was classic. I made sure I turned up the walkie-talkie so everyone could hear. "Simon's not even here. No."

Simple as that. No. I loved it because that's exactly what I said just minutes before.

I turned to madam Disney said, "You heard her. There's nothing else I can do."

Thirty seconds later I had a security guard hovering over me.

She left without putting up a fight and we both watched her pace in the parking lot for the next thirty minutes or so, yammering more and more animatedly into her cellphone. Every now and again she would throw up her free arm in anger, as if berating God – or maybe Walt – for letting her down.

I saw her again the following week and lo and behold there she was on the list, and miracle of miracles, she waited her turn in line. Boy was it painful for her when she sidled up to the table. There was a little war going on beneath her face, every muscle twitching as she struggled valiantly to be nice.

I loved it.

I mean loved loved loved it.

Yep, I admit it, I can be one petty son of a bitch.

It obviously wasn't that a big deal for Simon. Put it this way, no one ever said boo about any so-called missed meeting.

LOCATION, LOCATION, LOCATION

Not long after the Top 12 were picked for Season 3, they all moved into a mansion in the Hollywood Hills.

You'd imagine it would be conveniently located near the studio, right? It wasn't. It was actually the same place they used in the Los Angeles season of Donald Trump's Apprentice.

The house was a fucking mess.

Literally a giant dump.

The windows were cracked, the paint around them chipped and peeling. The walls weren't much better. It was picked by the executive producers based on pictures alone. No one actually went out to visit it so they didn't know what kind of condition it was in. Me, now I always thought the three key things in buying a property were location, location and location. So, along with a few other production assistants, I had to prep the house for the contestants, set up the beds, go grocery and supply shopping and do all of the day-to-day stuff that was needed to transform it into something habitable.

While we were setting up the beds and prepping the house, joints were being passed around, which in retrospect might explain why it took us so damned long to do what needed to be done, but we were all very mellow about it and didn't really give a shit that it was talking forever. We were out of the office.

The mansion itself was rather mysterious.

The owner only allowed us access to certain parts of the house, while other parts, including pretty much one entire area was locked and we had no access to it. Which of course only made me want to go poke around all the more.

Everything went well for the first few weeks, and then overnight, the shit started hitting the fan. Literally. The septic system started backing up in the front yard because there were so many people using the restrooms. Look at the numbers, in addition to the twelve contestants there were guardians and the security team who were there twenty-four seven, and then there were the producers and the reps from 19 Entertainment who stayed every single night. It's amazing the amount of crap that many people can crap. The septic system wasn't built for that much shit.

This, needless to say, generated plenty of drama between the production side of the show and the property owner. She blamed the show and the show blamed her. She would leave threatening messages on the production manager's voicemail pretty much daily. He recorded them all with a handheld mini-recorder that he kept near the phone. He was a wily old bastard. He'd set the phone to speakerphone when he talked and the recorder was always present. Now, I am not saying that he recorded phone calls, but the recorder was there, and let's put it this way, if he did, he broke all sorts of laws given it's illegal to record conversations in California without the consent of the other party.

This, incidentally, is why when Dr. Phil does his undercover investigations he charters a plane into Oregon, lands, and sits in the plane on the tarmac and makes his calls and records them without any issues. That's one of the many good things about Oregon, that and the no Sales Tax.

This dance with the homeowner went on and on and on, even after the show wrapped up for the season and we had completely moved out. She was adamant the show was responsible and demanded they foot the entire bill to fix the problem.

Things got pretty heated. At one point litigation was threatened. The production manager and Wylleen were getting ready to place yet another call to the homeowner when I just happened to walk by.

"Bucks!"

I did a one-eighty and stuck my head through the door. I was told to come in, close the door, and sit down. They told me that I was a witness in case this thing went to court. They wanted me to validate what had and hadn't been said by both parties. I really didn't want to be dragged into the middle of this.

Not even a little bit.

But, let's face it, there are a million other examples of how the executives use the rank and file however the hell they want, so why would this be any different? If you want to keep your job, you do what they say. That's just the way it is.

"I don't want any part of this," I said, only to be told to shut up, sit still and listen. I saw the mini-recorder beside the phone. I wouldn't be surprised if there's a tape languishing somewhere with my objection and their admonishment on it. I mean laws were broken everyday on the show, labor laws, code violations, drugs laws, and anything and everything in between. Why would they worry about a little thing like recording a phone call?

THE PORN HOUSE

I didn't hear much about the septic tank issues after that, but while they were dealing with that back at the office we were off exploring the rest of the house.

We were like Lewis and Clark. We broke into all of the locked rooms and went through every box and cupboard and drawer that we found. And we found a lot of them.

The house was a porn den. A little bit of background research revealed that the house had been used in several porn movies and had been wired up for live porn shows. We found cameras throughout the house. They were hidden in closets, hallways, bedrooms, we're talking a Big Brother porn house. What we couldn't work out was why cameras were set up in the closets.

Our best guess was that the house was used to stream live sex shows online. Like I said, Big Brother's voyeuristic house of porn kind of thing.

Girls would open the closet doors completely naked and in full view of the online world thanks to the cameras inside. It was rather amusing to think that the number one show on television was sharing a house with the remnants of a porn set.

And those boxes?

They were full of dildos, sex toys, movies, tubes of lube,

and all the paraphernalia of sex you'd need to shoot a hard-core flick. And of course we found a movie in which the house was easily recognizable.

A few of us watched clips in the office and looked at the stills. It was, without question, our house. It didn't surprise anyone when the Adderall-addicted porn-surfer head production manager found the movie and alerted us to it. Ironically we'd all suspected him of being in porn before joining the show, and wondered about him getting into it after he was booted from the show.

And then another tape surfaced, one which might well have backed up our suspicions about Adderall porn surfer. Someone was sent to Wylleen's friend's place to pick up the tape so we could all gather round to watch it and see if we could ID him.

I didn't watch the tape. I made excuses. And no one told me if it was him or not because they knew I wasn't interested.

Of course, while all the talk was porn-centric one of the security guards, a decent guy not much older than me, admitted that he had 'starred' in a porno, a gangbang shoot where he was 'treated' to a little oral.

Yep, these were the people I was working with. Porn stars and drug addicts. Classy.

THE SEXUAL HARASSMENT SEMINAR

Out of the blue we were called to a sexual harassment meeting.

Theater-style seating was set up for this as well as a projector screen.

This was a full on comedy stuff.

Nigel and Ken were in the back of the group cracking jokes and generally being wise-asses laughing the entire time. The trickle-down effect meant that because they didn't give a shit, nobody else did. Of course, the fact that the woman running the meeting was dressed in a skin-tight pink patent leather outfit that offered a fairly lurid anatomy lesson, didn't help either. You could almost see the blood pulse through her camel toe, the thing was that tight. How anyone was supposed to focus on anything she said when she dressed like a Santa Monica Boulevard hooker was beyond me. That she was trying to explain the ins and outs of sexual harassment was the kind of juxtaposition that could only happen in Hollywood.

There were to distinct types of reaction going on, polarizing the atmosphere in the room. The guys, mostly from the security set up, were all giddy and titillated while the women were mortified by the beaver fever going on.

Texts were zipping around fast and furious. Giggles.

Laughter. Crude jokes whispered behind hands. But all credit to her, she soldiered on through the innuendo, veiled, and not so veiled, being thrown out from the back of the crowd.

If I'm honest, I can't remember a damned thing she said. All I can remember, and with vivid eye-burning-out clarity, is her poor vagina being cut in two by the pink patent leather just a few feet from my face.

THE EGG SALAD SANDWICH INCIDENT

I haven't really told you much about Wylleen, so it's about time I did something about that.

She was an animal.

I know I haven't told you her industry nickname was "Cunt" or "Hollywood Cunt" but as vulgar and disgusting as the word cunt is, and believe me I don't use it lightly, I don't think it comes even remotely close to capturing just how vile she was, nor how badly she treated people.

She was an uglier version of the Queen of Hearts from Lewis Carroll's Alice, one misstep and it would be off with your head.

Not long after the season started I was asked by Wylleen's assistant if I had time to run over to the CBS commissary and grab her some lunch – specifically an egg salad sandwich. On the scale of nuclear physicist down to garbage technician Egg Salad Sandwich Buyer didn't register so much as a little Geiger-blip. It was only an egg salad sandwich for fuck's sake. What could go wrong? Famous last words, though not particularly ones I'd pick for my tombstone. I grabbed the post-it note from her assistant along with some cash and made my way down the back stairs and around to the main building at the CBS studio lot where the commissary was located. I stood in line and waited my turn to order, per the post-it note, an egg salad sandwich on wheat bread. Simple. I placed the order and thought nothing else of it. Again simple. I grabbed the sandwich and made my way to the register to pay before heading back to the office to bust my ass to make everyone else rich. Job done, I placed the sandwich on the assistant's desk. She was on the phone and I wasn't comfortable as last man on the totem pole approaching the head of the production, even with Egg Salad Sandwich offering in hand. Her assistant waved me over to her desk just as I had sat down at mine so I got up and made my way back over. She had scribbled on her legal yellow pad asking me to take the sandwich into the boss's office, but to make sure that I knocked first and to wait until I heard the word "yes" or something along those lines which would let me know that it was now my turn to let her know that I had her food.

It was an elaborate dance for a damned sandwich, but ours is not to reason why, as the poem goes. Ours is just to do and die...

So, by now my palms were sweaty, and I was obviously nervous.

I had never said a word to her or even looked in her direction, as everyone else appeared to be so damn afraid of her. It's Basic Office Survival Skills, do what all the seasoned employees of the show do. Act busy when she walks in in the morning, head down when she's out of her personal office prowling about like a lioness in her office Serengeti. I hesitated, looking at her door. Then, biting the bullet, knocked on the frame.

Waiting, waiting, waiting.

Finally after what seemed like an eternity she said "Yes", to which I responded "I have your sandwich, may I enter." So far so good. She said yes so I walked into the office and placed the sandwich on the corner of her desk.

I turned around and walked out.

I'd survived.

She hadn't even bothered to lift her eyes from her computer screen, let alone say thank you.

It didn't matter. I was out. Free at last. Free at last. Ahem. Sorry about that.

I went back to my desk but no more than a minute later I heard this banshee-like wail from her office, "Who ordered this sandwich for me? Get them in here now!"

I could of, and I am sure I almost did, shit myself. Just a little bit.

It wasn't going to be pretty.

I looked at her assistant's face. There was this mix of fear/sadness/anger written all over it. My testicles crawled up inside my stomach as I stood up. Like the condemned man but without the hearty breakfast (without even the offending Egg Salad Sandwich), I made my way slowly to her office. I had to force myself knock, while saying a slight prayer to the God of Myocardial Infarctions to help me out this once, and waited for her to either keel over clutching her chest or tell me to come in.

I was shit out of luck.

She said yes so I walked in, still hoping Myocardial guy would help me out in the next four or five seconds... Sweat broke out on my brow, and my face had flushed bright red. I stood in front of her desk.

"Explain," she said.

The sandwich container was in was open in front of her. It was surreal. The whole thing threw me for a loop. I felt like I had walked into some surrealist play: when is a sandwich not a sandwich?

With Myocardial God having let me down so badly, I had no choice but to tell her that I'd been asked by her assistant to go to the commissary and get an egg salad sandwich on wheat for her, which, as she could see, was exactly what I had done. All the requisite parts of the sandwich were there, the egg, the salad, the wheat bread. All that remained was to accept the beat down:

"Who the fuck told you to make the sandwich? Huh? I didn't want anything made! I wanted to do it myself. I wanted to put the ingredients together myself. Remember that for next time. And I didn't want a tomato, who the fuck told you to get a tomato? Jesus Fucking Christ, I've fired people over things like this before. Now fuck off."

It was almost laughable in a sense. Here was this massive Jabba the Hutt of a woman screaming at me over a tomato and an egg salad sandwich – and on what planet is it normal to order an unmade sandwich? It only becomes a damned sandwich when it is put together, that's how John Montagu, the Fourth Earl of Sandwich created it after all. He didn't think, hmm, let's just put all these ingredients side by side on the plate.

I thought I was special, but "The Egg Salad Incident" was a staple of more than just her diet. It was a regular thing. A few years after this happened I was talking to another former employee, discussing how working on the show was bullshit, the usual, and I happened to mention the "Egg Salad Incident". Lo and behold, he had the same thing happen to him, right down to the filling. I guess she was bored, or vindictive... or vindictively bored... or maybe just a cunt. That was probably it.

SIT AND WAIT

The show was in full swing by this point, and I was spending more and more time with the contestants. I had gotten close to a few of the parents of the underage contestants who were along as chaperones, and it wasn't long before they were sharing their feelings with me.

With all the so-called showbiz, the glitz and the glam that was promised by Tinsel Town and the Hollywood Dream, they were bored out of their minds. Because, well, it wasn't like that. It wasn't glitz. It wasn't glam. All they did, day in day out was sit and wait, sit and wait, sit and wait. While their children were on stage going through rehearsals, they sat and watched. While they were getting their hair and make-up done, they sat and watched. While they went shopping for outfits, they sat and watched. While they filmed music videos on the weekend for the show's sponsors, they sat and watched. You see a pattern emerging here?

And me, I was going a little crazy on their behalf.

The vast majority of the chats I had with the guardians revolved around the fact that they really didn't feel that the show was being honest or forthcoming with information. Promises were being made on a daily basis. Promises were made to the guardians and contestants to shut them up while the show figured out other ways to exploit their kids and make as much money as possible. The guardians, one in particular, who I got along with very well and grew close, to felt that the show was basically a joke. See, she remembered all of the promises. She remembered being told by the producers that her child would be allowed two complete days off a week to do as they pleased, meaning they could have two days of 'reality'. Of course they'd have to have a bodyguard in tow wherever they went. Or they would have, if it had lasted and they'd been allowed to venture outside into the 'real world'. There was no such thing as reality for these guys. Something new was being manufactured every single day of the week. Rehearsals, shopping, photo shoots, recording, interviews, and on and on and on.

If they were really lucky they got one full day off a week.

Another major complaint this parent had – and one that was echoed by future contestants as the season went on – was how the executive producers had a major say in the songs that were performed. Everyone had been lead to believe that they could choose whatever song they wanted, off of a pre-approved list of course, for their performance song on Tuesday's.

This was true, if the truth could be stretched like giant sticky taffy and still be called true.

On Thursday's the contestants would start picking their songs with the help of Michael Orland and Byrd, the vocal and music coaches. If Michael wasn't hitting on you that was only because he was hitting on someone else, and Byrd though she was a gift from the Kalliope herself, meaning she was just that bit better than everybody else in the room. By the time she started commuting back and forth between the United States and Canada working on both versions of Idol it was amazing we could find a room big enough to contain her ego.

FAVORITISM?

As Thursday rolled around the production assistants all knew that one or more of us were going to be stuck in the office until the early morning hours. That was just the way it was.

The contestants all got one-on-one time with both Michael and Byrd, but the way this one-on-one was meted out wasn't exactly equal. Put it this way, one contestant could practice with them for an hour or so, while another received four hours with them. Anyone could see that this arrangement gave an unfair advantage to certain contestants. The fair thing would have been for each of them to get exactly the same allotted one-on-one time every Thursday regardless of whatever song they choose. But who said Idol was fair? Not me.

It should come as no surprise that as the season went by contestants began to see the favoritism for what it was. And it really ought to come as even less of a surprise to learn that the ones getting the special treatment were the standouts. The better they were, the more time they got.

Equal time was only one of the issues people had with song selection Thursday. Some of the contestants had their songs picked for them regardless of what they had been rehearsing with Byrd and Michael Orland. Yep, you read that right, some of the contestants weren't allowed to sing the songs that they had officially picked and been rehearsing all week.

I'll let that sink in for a second.

Here you've got one of the most important moments in these guy's lives to date, going up on stage in front of all of America's eyes, and at the last minute they're getting their songs yanked from under them.

How could it happen, you ask?

Well, facts are facts, and those facts had names. Their names were Nigel and Ken. These guys had a huge hand in the songs that the contestants sang. First of all they put the lists together with the help of the shows music supervisor, based on what songs she was able to clear the rights to for the week. This level of influence included the show's themes from week to week, the special guest judges, the works. Nigel and Ken were ever-presents during song selection day. They'd typically go up to the room together, sit in and watch, and make suggestions to the contestants. These suggestions were, more often than not, more than simply suggestions. The contestants weren't happy with this, obviously, I mean, would you be? A few of them weren't afraid to say it, at least not privately. Saying so to Nigel and Ken was a different matter.

Of course many of them felt as though they'd been lied to from day one as far as how things were going to go, what they'd be expected to do, and simple stuff like time off, this just served to add another layer to the tension that was already simmering away. As the season went on the simmering turned slowly to a boil.

It carried on into Season 4 as well.

Unsurprisingly, the contestants wanted to sing the song they had chosen, and remember this was from a list supplied by the show, but they were pressured into changing their numbers through comment and innuendo couched as 'suggestions' by Nigel and Ken.

And when they would not take the 'suggestions'? Well, one contestant admitted that Nigel and Ken grew so frustrated with their refusal to just sing the damned song the show wanted them to sing they point blank refused them the right to their song choice, telling the contestant, "No. You're not singing that song and that's final. This is the one you're singing."

Of course the contestants didn't dare talk back. If they fought too hard, or questioned their motives, it would only make their position on the show untenable and they'd no doubt find themselves being voted out in the not too distant future. So much for being able to stand up for yourself.

From the first moment I learned the truth about the song selection process I had my suspicions. Things were done for reasons. What is it they're always looking for on crime shows? Means, motive and method. Well the show certainly had the means, and given the sheer amount of money at stake, there was motive. Method? Well, if you interfere with song selection it's easy to weight the deck and make sure the preferred contestant gets the crowd-pleasing song, isn't it? And if the contestant was making waves, asking questions, pressing for rights or just not being the perfect little servant tugging the forelock and bowing and scraping while they waited to be trotted out and patted on the head just enough to encourage them to perform their tricks? Well, it wasn't too difficult for the producers inflict a terrible song on them, was it?

Idol was proving to be a little like Shrek's onion, the more layers you peeled away the more your eyes watered, and each new layer only served to reinforce the idea that the whole thing was one giant money-making sham.

Let's not beat about the bush here, every week on the job brought new revelations, and those revelations convinced me of one unassailable fact, *American Idol* was a complete fake.

YOUR LIFE OR YOUR JOB – CHOOSE WISELY

During the Season I had an appointment with my dermatologist. Being out in the blistering sun for prolonged stretches was catching up with me in the form of moles and freckles on over my body.

I had some worrying ones on my back. They just looked odd so I wanted to have them checked out, if only to put my mind at rest. Most of us have got over-active imaginations when it comes to issues of mortality. The only way to shut the ragged beast up is with the truth. So I made the appointment and informed the production manager, and when the time came, went to my appointment.

The dermatologist took small samples of any and all questionable moles he found, including several on my back, one on my chest, one on my inner thigh, and one on my left temple. It was going to take a few days to get the results, which given the sheer number of samples he'd taken meant a few days out of my mind with worry, my imagination running wild.

Even better, he told me there would probably be a good chance that I would need to see him for a follow up because he believed that some of them appeared to be abnormal cell structures, but he needed the results to be sure.

I told the production manager that it looked like I'd have

to go back and see the doctor in a few days because he suspected some of my moles could be cancerous. He said that was fine and just to let him know. So I waited by the phone, and man I hated waiting for the hammer to fall. My mind was going through all the permutations, running the numbers, worrying and worrying some more, then finally the phone rang and the dermatologist had been right on the money, most of the moles had returned an abnormal cell structure.

Instead of seeing him again, he recommended that I go to a plastic surgeon in Encino and just have the moles excised, in full. Once that was done he'd send them to the lab to make sure that they'd removed all the abnormal cells. That was scheduled for the following week and once again I told the production manager who was fine with everything. So I went the plastic surgeon and he proceeded to slice and dice my moles as efficiently as Dad slicing through the Christmas ham.

The cuts left gaping holes all over my body.

I don't know what I'd expected, but I hadn't expected that.

But, morbid fascination in full-on killed-the-cat mode, I asked him if I could watch him cut out the one from the middle of chest. He said sure and set me up at an angle where I could see what he was doing.

It was odd. I mean odd like an out-of-body experience odd. Here was a guy just carving away at my skin and I couldn't feel a thing. I kept thinking of all those urban legends where people wake up and their one of their kidneys have been cut out as I watched the blood bubble up to fill the wounds that he'd just made. It was grotesquely fascinating. Then he stitched me up, rather loosely, explaining that there was a good chance I would have to see him the following week if any of the moles or the skin around them showed signs of abnormal cell structure. It wasn't so much the moles at this point, it was more about the surrounding skin and if the abnormalities had spread.

So, more of that waiting, more of that interminable worrying, and more of that morbid imagination running wild.

I finally got the phone call: it felt like the worst possible news, the skin around the moles on my back had 'questionable' cell structure. He didn't say abnormal. Questionable. I was going to have to go back in and have more skin peeled off my back. I told the production manager about this and again he said it was fine, not to worry about it, this was my health, so get it taken care of.

The day before I had to go in, I went to find him, just to remind him what was going on, as I didn't want any unpleasant surprises. He wasn't in the office that day so I told Wylleen instead.

"Well, you need to be in the office by 10 a.m. because you have wristbands to hand out."

I did an almost comical double-take. I won't tell you what I said, because I can't remember what I said, I was so dumbfounded. I mean, seriously, there was a very real possibility that I had melanoma and that it could have spread without me knowing it. And there she was, the Hollywood Cunt telling me she didn't give a shit about my 'minor' surgery or possible skin cancer, she wanted me out there in the sun come 10 a.m. to hand out their precious fucking wristbands, gaping holes and all. I wondered if she'd be willing to come out and drain the pus and blood throughout the day?

I was stunned, but at the same time I knew she was drop-dead serious.

Serious enough to fire me if I didn't get back to the office in time to distribute those fucking wristbands.

The show must go on, right?

So what if the performing monkey's dripping blood and pus and fresh from the operating table?

PAULA'S NOSE

One thing that always struck me as mighty peculiar for a 'live reality show' was the fact that the whole thing was scripted. We aren't talking a few gags timed to slip in between the laugh track. An entire script was put together, copies were made and then distributed amongst the producers and the rest of the crew on the morning of the show.

The script supervisor for the show (yep the show had a script supervisor) met with the producers on a regular basis and sat in on the majority of performances.

It was their responsibility to make sure the show stuck as close to the script as possible, time it so that Ryan was on his mark when he needed to say this or to do that, and that the contestants entered and exited the stage on cue. It was a smooth well-oiled machine, but it wasn't reality. At least not in my book. I don't see how something that is scripted from start to finish can qualify as reality.

Of course it wasn't alone in this loose interpretation of reality.

During my time in Los Angeles I worked on several reality programs and live events and, hand on heart, each and every one of them was carefully scripted. And post Idol, the other reality shows I worked on were entirely scripted. Everything was staged. From the shopping excursions to the "mayhem" that the stars found themselves involved with, the so-called family drama, the conflict, the surprise sucker-punches, the shocking revelations, they were all concocted by the show's producers to feed the gossip mags and generate ratings. How else would they keep dull families and their inane chatter appealing?

Step back next time you tune in, look at what you're seeing and think about it for a moment and you can practically see the transitions in the script, the joins and the dreadful acting. These shows are about as real as Paula Abdul's nose.

DON'T SNEEZE. IT'S NOT IN THE SCRIPT

During the Monday before each show the script supervisor would typically be found sitting just off-stage watching the rehearsals, taking times and noting when the contestants entered and exited the stage, working out the precise time when Ryan needed to do his intros and all that jazz.

Once the rehearsals wrapped for the day the meetings began. He'd sit with the senior and supervising producers and between them they'd square away everything and put the finishing touches on the final script.

Typically it's the supervising producer who writes all of Ryan's dialogue. All the corny jokes, all the stupid puns, they're not Ryan's rapier wit and dazzling repartee, they're all courtesy of the show's supervising producer. I guess the show would be better categorized as a scripted series with amateur talent, but even amateur is a stretch for a lot of them given that several of them have had prior record deals, management deals, and even recorded albums before they set foot on the stage.

It was the job of one production assistant to stay late every Monday night and take the final script when it was complete to the "drop box" in Studio City.

The drop box consisted of a rubber storage shed in the parking lot behind an old commercial building. All of the cloak and dagger was like something out of an old Bogart movie, The Maltese Falcon maybe, or The Big Sleep. I could see myself as Philip Marlowe doing the night drive to the drop box. The directions were always secured to the script with a rubber band telling the printer how many copies we needed and when we needed then done by. We'd throw the script into the shed, close the door, and leave for the night. And by night I mean ten or eleven, sometimes even midnight. And if things were especially hairy in the office, well after midnight. I think the latest I ever dropped a script off was around three in the morning. Then as if by magic we'd return around six or seven in the morning and collect the copies of the final script and give them to the script coordinator to distribute to whoever needed one.

The final script is thick. We're talking a hundred plus pages, and word for word, act by act, it's all laid out in black and white.

Of course the final script had to be delivered to Ryan's house the night before the show, so usually the guy doing the "drop box" run to Studio City would deliver a second copy to Ryan's house on the way.

And equally of course, we couldn't just walk up to the door and ring the bell. Hollywood celebs need their quirks right? Otherwise they'd just be normal people. With Ryan we were supposed to zip in and zip out, leaving it leaning - not laying on the ground - up against the front door. Don't ask me why everything had to be so anal, I couldn't tell you. That's just how it was. And when I took over the duties as production coordinator I continued with the tradition of leaning not laying when I sent the production assistants deliver the script. After all, maybe it had some sort of cabalistic significance, how was I supposed to know?

This was one of those little bugbears that made me wonder if the show was fixed. Did they write twelve possible endings, then eleven, then ten, like they were scripting Ten Green Bottles and each week one more had accidentally fallen? I mean a full script was written and signed on off on for every live show, but if the outcome was supposed to be reliant upon the viewer's votes, how can they possibly cover all of the eventualities in a script?

That always made me wonder if all of those phone-in votes that cost the viewer's millions of dollars a season were ever actually counted, and even if they were, if they had any impact upon who went home and who went through to the next round?

REHEARSING THOSE "OFF THE CUFF" COMMENTS

While we're contemplating the notion of the show being scripted, it shouldn't come as a huge surprise to learn that most, if not all, of Simon's comments are pre-scripted. The difference was that he wrote them himself.

During the show days it was typical that Paula and Randy would show up almost to the minute when we went live, jumped into wardrobe and had a final hair and make-up touch up, then headed out to the judges table.

Simon, on the other hand, would spend a lot of time at the studio on Tuesdays. Holed up in his dressing room, he'd watch the final dress rehearsals on a monitor he'd had installed in the room when they were being put together. It wasn't exactly a state secret that he sat in his dressing room, hunched over his smokeless ashtray (he wasn't allowed to smoke inside the CBS studios, but he did anyway and was caught plenty of times), taking notes on the final dress rehearsal performances.

Did you really think he was that fast on his feet? Did you honestly think his dry, witty, and oh so snarky comments were off the cuff? Sure, he's smart, sure he knows what's what and has an eye for talent, and yep, he's a genuine hard ass, but he most certainly isn't as witty as you'd think from watching the show.

I've never saw the actual notes, but give me another reason for him sitting there studying the rehearsal performances, given that they are identical to the live show down to the hair, make-up, wardrobe, and songs? Pre-writing his judgments lets him come up with the most scandalous sound bites sure to blow-up in the media the following morning. It's a great way to nurture his image, be it the image of him as the bad guy, the nice guy, or the only one who actually makes a blind bit of sense. The guy's no fool. He's media savvy and loves the Press and the scandals that go along with show every bit as much as the producers do.

So, if you held a gun to my head and said Bucks, pick, yes or no, does Simon write his comments pre-show, there's no two ways about it for me. It's just my opinion, and we've already established that opinions are like assholes, right?

WE'RE ALMOST DONE (WOULD I LIE?)

As Season 3 progressed you didn't need to be psychic to tell just how frustrated the contestants and guardians were becoming with the stupidly long days and the insane amount of junkets and, well, frankly, junk they had to put up with.

The most commonly voiced questions were "Are we almost done?" and "How much longer?" Being around the contestants all the time I was one of the ones who kept asking these questions. On any given day they were almost always quarantined on the third floor of the CBS studio. It sounds ridiculous to say quarantined. It makes it sound as though their newfound fame was some sort of contagious disease. They were kept isolated from most of what was going on around them, shepherded off into a holding room. The room came complete with snacks and beverages, a mini craft service area just for them, with couches and chairs, board games and video games. This was where they hung out when they were in the studio – which was pretty much all day every day. They would sit there trying to keep themselves occupied with the bare minimum of stuff the show provided them with.

Staff did their best to stay away from this area as much as possible while the contestants were around, though security was never far away, the rest of us tried to keep our distance until we were needed.

If the producers wanted one of the contestants for a photo shoot or some other promotional doh-dah they would just pop their head in the door and tell them to jump. Until then, they just had to sit around and twiddle their thumbs. We always knew the schedule – it was posted throughout the studio every morning – but never where the contestants or their guardians might see it. Sure, every now and then they would run across one of the schedules, but for the most part the production assistants, at the demand of the producers, kept it under wraps. They wanted people kept in the dark.

The schedule was broken down by hour and subject, and would be marked with stuff like: "Photo shoot. 11:00am-2:00pm" The times on these schedules were pretty arbitrary, and save for show days never met.

And whenever I was asked those questions, the 'are we done yet' ones, my answer was always the same. Almost. Yep, you got it, I lied to the contestants every day because my bosses told me to.

WOULD I LIE? (AGAIN?)

Things change. People's willingness to help changes. People's interest declines. A classic example of this would be the fact that when I started working on the show I'd do my best to get answers to every question that I was asked. If I didn't know, invariably I knew someone who did, so I'd seek them out and ask. Sometimes it would be another production assistant, other times it would fall to a producer to answer.

At the start of the season the general excitement levels were high, everyone was eager and enthused, so the answers were genuine and honest. By mid-season stress levels were way up and willingness to answer way down, as though they were pivoting on some seesaw. Eventually I was told to just tell them whatever would make them shut up. Anything for a quiet life. So I started getting creative, making up answers that were bald faced lies.

If I knew that there were still several hours to go before they'd be needed, my canned response was, "Oh, don't worry we're really close to being done." Then a few hours later someone would track me down and ask again, to which canned response number two was to explain the wait away with, "They're having some technical difficulties downstairs so it's taking a lot longer than they thought it would take, sorry about this."

It was amazing how many 'technical difficulties' took place every day to make sure the schedule basically ran smoothly. I got very good at coming up with suitably vague technical glitches. So good, in fact, you'd think we'd been feeding our Gremlins after midnight.

The show seemed to go to great lengths to keep the contestants in the dark. For instance, contestants were never allowed to enter the office. If they needed anything they had to wait until a staff member was around and ask them for help.

I won't pretend that I particularly enjoyed lying to the guys, but I became really rather proficient at it. Forget silver-tongue, mine was forked. I could lie with the best of them, but hell, I knew that if I told the truth I'd be fired, no questions asked, for breaking the party line. I mean, Heaven forbid anyone actually knew what the fuck was going on, right? It's not like they were adults or had a right to know why they'd been herded off into a room and left to rot for hours on end. Because, that way, my friends, lay madness for the producers. Madness, worked up talent and serious butt-pain.

JOHN AND KATE PLUS EIGHTY

The contestants had their own coordinator, a position rather creatively called Contestant Coordinator. The contestant coordinator handled their schedules and dealt with any issues that arose specifically concerning the contestants. We're talking about one of the most annoying jobs in the crew—it demanded a lot of time and attention, hell, it was a 24/7 job. There was no such thing as a private life for the contestant coordinator. They were on hand day and night for months. They lived with the contestants. They babysat the contestants. The chaperoned and mollycoddled them. They fetched. They carried. They shadowed.

If they were lucky, the contestant coordinator got to go home maybe once a week to collect the mail, pay the bills and get a change of clothes.

One person was in charge of the constants new lives.

Hard to imagine how that could be any fun, isn't it?

John and Kate Plus Eight? Forget it. This was John sans Kate with a bonus set of quadruplets and all of their friends too for shits and giggles...

DIANE'S MOTHER

With all that pent up frustration and nervous energy it shouldn't come as any surprise that people needed a release valve every now and again, a way to just blow it off. Nine times out of ten that release came in the form of narcotics.

As I've already intimated, most of us smoked pot during the days, while some folks snorted coke. It was our valve.

Now, during this entire time the mother of Diana Degarmo was a constant pain in the ass, and not only the contestant coordinator's butt, but every other butt she came into contact with. That's a lot of buts (or butts) in one sentence. Unfortunately we couldn't just get a suppository to take care of her. She was a sneak. There's no nice way of saying it. She was always up to something. Scheming. Manipulating.

She started out nice, hell I'd go so far as to say very nice, but it didn't take long for the make-up to wear off and reveal the ugly-assed monster beneath. She was your typical stage mother. You know the sort, loud, screechy and more than likely living off of her daughter. It was painful to watch the way she treated her, but it wasn't like we hadn't seen it all before. She just personified all of the worst aspects of 'Stage Mom' in one nasty little package. She started off cornering production assistants and asking them if they had any information that they could give her to help her understand what was coming up down the road.

Innocent enough, right?

Of course it doesn't take Rainman to realize she was fishing for themes, music nights, basically anything that would give Diana a leg up in the competition. Two minutes to Jeopardy indeed.

Of course she was nice to our faces because she knew that we held the keys to the kingdom. We had the information she wanted. We also wound up spending more time with her than anyone else on the show. And then it was like a switch flicked somewhere in the dark recesses of her mind and Stage Mom mutated into Hell Diva.

She could no longer ride in the 15 passenger van with the other contestants. Apparently it was too hard for her to get her lardy ass in and out of, and just for good measure she started to suffer from motion sickness. Sure, the Hollywood Hills are serpentine, loads of narrow streets twisting and turning left and right, so on the surface it sounded quite reasonable. Her suggestion was that she rent a car and follow on behind us wherever we went in the passenger van. Of course her daughter would have to stay in the van with us because she was only allowed to ride in show vehicles.

So, the next day Diva Lady turned up in a fairly new (if not brand spanking new) Mercedes. It was a lovely shade of silver-gray, compliments of her daughter's bank account, no doubt.

I guess she wanted to look the part for the short drive to and from the mansion, after all the rest of the time she was supposed to be sitting at the studio while Diana rehearsed, posed for photos and all that hoopla. As Diana's guardian she had to be present at all times, so it wasn't like she had the opportunity to actually drive the Merc anywhere, was it?

Of course, she would often disappear for a few hours at a time, even after being told again and again that she wasn't allowed to do so. She was always trying to pawn the responsibilities of caring for Diana off on the other guardians, using excuses like she wasn't feeling well or had errands to run. She'd claim she'd been asking the show's producers to do things, but her requests always fell on deaf ears, which was, frankly, bullshit. If contestants (or for that matter, their guardians) needed anything the show got it for them pronto. That was one thing the show was good at. More than once, the other guardians would vent about Diana's mother. It wasn't funny, but it was laughable, if that makes sense.

Eventually Diana's mom ditched the charade and just left the studio whenever she felt like it. She'd be needed for something or other, and wouldn't be around. Whenever this happened we would have to go in search of the silver Mercedes. It was, more often than not, like looking for the Holy bloody Grail, but without Dan Brown to guide us.

All employees had parking passes that we'd display in our vehicles when we arrived for the day so the CBS security team knew we were allowed to be there. Somehow Diana's mom finagled one. No one really knew how she did it, but she proudly displayed it, bold as brass. Staff members also had security badges with our pictures on them that we would have to scan when we arrived in the morning that would allow the gates to open so we could get into the parking lot. Security was pretty tight. We had to display them whenever we were on the CBS lot. No one ever really knew how Diana's mom managed to get in and out at will when everyone else was basically locked up like inmates on Rikers Island. She must have had some sort of ninja super power.

The producers grew ever so tired of her. I mean it got to

the point where they were actively hoping that Diana would get voted off and that it would happen soon. They banned us from interacting with her. We were to avoid her at all times and only interact when we absolutely had to. There would be no conversations beyond the succinct delivery of the information we had to tell her. We were not allowed to answer any of her questions. There were to be no updates about the day. We weren't to answer questions, even inane ones like how much longer we had left for the day. We were to keep her in the dark. A box would have been more fun, but hey-ho.

As you would expect, this bugged the hell out of her. She knew something was up. She stewed for a while, and then did what we all knew she would do. It was a cardinal sin, a giant no-no on the show. She got hold of one of the contact lists, which included the contact information, email, phone number, and quite often the home address of every single employee who had anything to do with the show. We're talking all of the Fox and FremantleMedia employees.

And what did she do with that fool's gold? You know what she did, don't you? You can see the train wreck coming from a mile away, can't you? Yep, she was stupid enough to send out a mass email to all of the executives and higher ups whining about how she was being harassed and abused by the show's employees and how she wasn't afraid to tell anyone about it. Anyone, of course, was a great blanket threat that included the media.

Being at the bottom of the totem pole at the time I didn't get to read the actual email, but plenty of others in the office did, and more than one of them delighted in sharing the details. As you can imagine, this did not sit well with the higher ups. A meeting was called. The way I heard the story they were most displeased that she had gotten a hold of the contact list given that they were off limits to anyone but show employees. How she did was anyone's guess. Maybe someone left one lying around and she snatched it, or maybe she snuck into the office and grabbed one? After all, if you stood at the office door you could clearly see the brightly colored contact lists just 20 feet away. Maybe the temptation was just too great for her? Either way, security was told to keep a close eye on her. And boy did they. Everyone did. Every step she made, every breath she took, no one trusted her a damned bit.

And, surprise surprise, she quickly got wise to this and set out to make things as difficult as possible.

The dressing room set up was fairly standard: typically the male contestants got two dressing rooms connected by a single bathroom, and likewise for the females, meaning they all had to crowd into these small dressing rooms. They were packed in like sardines, and it was made worse with the guardians taking up precious room. Knowing that Diana was a front runner along with Fantasia, Mother Degarmo decided that she would transform one entire dressing room into a "Diana Room" where she put up newspaper articles, pictures, the works, plastering them all over the walls to create a Diana shrine, and spouting some bullshit about how this room was for her and Diana, and no one else was allowed in.

She started to isolate herself and Diana from everyone else, and in true Svengali fashion went as far as to monitor what Diana ate. Supposedly Mommy Dearest would only allow Diana a single piece of "junk food" from the craft service table. Thankfully that wasn't my problem.

The woman could balance chips the size of a small military junta on her shoulders. She made no secret of how much she despised the contestant coordinator because he never gave in to her constant niggley little demands. Imagine everyone's mock surprise when she accidentally "found" drugs in his toiletry bag. Allegedly it was marijuana and cocaine. So, ignoring the question of how she got hold of his bag, let's just imagine her tiptoeing around the studio until she found it (which wasn't unheard of. I ran into her in the middle of off-limit hallways and she'd always say she just needed to get up and get moving) because I like the image of her skulking from shadow to shadow like some big cat stalking her game. After her drug find, a meeting was held and the contest coordinator was 'fired' and told that he would never work for the show or any other FremantleMedia production. The inverted commas are lurking around the word fired for a reason. Days after the season wrapped he was back in the loop.

I can think of plenty of ways you could interpret this story, but given what I saw on a daily basis with the rampant drug use in the office I know how my two and two would be put together.

SHE'S FREE AT LAST

I remember during the Greensboro auditions for Season 5 Diana showed up and made it a point to tell all of male employees, especially the producers she remembered from her time on the show that she was free of her mom. She had turned eighteen, the age of majority. It was mildly amusing to say the least. She obviously knew just how much we didn't love her mom.

THERE'S ANOTHER ONE BORN EVERY DAY

One of Season 3's standout, smart-ass moments, courtesy of yours truly, happened just outside the elephant door—a giant rolling shutter that lead into the holding area and onto the sound stage area.

I was bored and had no one in my credential line so I decided to spice things up a bit and just see how stupid and gullible people really were. Bad of me, I know. Wicked Bucks. Just plain wicked. I made my way over to the elephant door and stood there. I didn't say anything. I just looked up into the sky and used my hand to shield my eyes from the sun. It didn't take more than a couple minutes of me standing there, staring upwards, before one of the show's photographers (a real space cadet of a woman, but absolutely lovely with it) approached me and asked what I was doing. She wasn't just lovely, she was hot. Hell, she had been on Baywatch wearing the red bathing suit, running in slow motion with the yellow float and blond locks flowing in the Los Angeles beach air. So, yep, that counts as hot in my book. Hot and just a little bit dumb to go along with the blond.

Without taking my hand from my face and looking at her I asked, "Do you see that up there?"

She didn't have a clue what I was looking at because, obviously, there was nothing up there to look at, just a few clouds, which were a rarity in the L.A. sky. She mirrored my pose, bracing her camera with her other hand, and stood there staring up at the clouds.

"You that mean thing right there?" she asked.

I said, "Yes, yes, you can see it."

"Oh, my gosh yes, it's like it's hiding behind the clouds." She said.

Doing my best not to laugh, and chewing just a little bit at my lower lip, I nodded solemnly and said, "Yes, that's what I was thinking."

We stood there for a few more minutes and during that time a couple of camera guys and show gaffers joined the crowd. It was perfect. Priceless. I couldn't have planned it better. Having her there beside me was brilliant. She was just gullible enough to play into my game and give it all the credibility I needed to pull it off. She was always a bundle of excited energy, yammering on about anything and everything that's going on.

"Look, it's behind the cloud. We don't know what it is," she blurted out as they sidled up, like some kind of news reporter breaking a story live on the air. Only, of course, there was no story.

By this point, anyone who showed up got into position with their hand over their eyes, shielding them from the sun so they could get a better view of what wasn't up there. From a distance it probably looked as though we were all saluting some Big Wig. I could imagine passersby thinking Simon Cowell liked to play soldiers.

More and more people had gathered, drawn to the crowd, including an executive from Fox who rolled up in their SUV and gawked at the group as we were all gawking up at the sky. The gawking was contagious. He got out of the car and made his way over to crowd, which had grown to a good twenty people or so.

Now, if you believed the cloud gazers, there were two objects in the air where really there were none. I guess it was some sort of mass hallucination. The photographer finally decided to try to capture some of the bizarre unidentified flying objects with her camera and started snapping away. Then zoom into the non-existent objects on her camera. According to her one was greenish, the other red, and after few more shots she thought she saw a silverish one lurking behind the others.

I seriously couldn't believe that people were buying into the make believe, because there was nothing and I mean nada, zip, zilch, in the sky save for the clouds. But not only were they buying into it, they were feeding it, adding details.

I guess you could say I brainwashed the crowd. I told people what they wanted to hear. Some had to leave the group because they needed to get back to their camera or audio duties, but for the most part everyone stood there, saluting the sky. Whenever the clouds moved even a little a bit everyone would make the same noise, a slight gasp, as though the non-existent UFOs were going to suddenly be revealed. I was really struggling by now and had to slope off to one side. I stopped watching the sky and watched them as they threw out all these whack-job conspiracy theories about what was going on above us.

"They hid behind the clouds," or "They're making the clouds to cover their visit our planet," and "They're up there, spying on us."

Only in California, my friends, only in California.

There's a reason L Ron built his church here.

People had cellphone cameras out and were snapping away

along with the photographer, who swore (I promise I'm not making this shit up) over and over that she could see them in her viewfinder. Hell, if she could, good for her, but I suspect maybe bad for the show, given she was imaging Little Green Men.

Maybe it was Xenu?

After about twenty minutes of the charade I grew tired and headed inside to grab a snack from the craft service table before wrapping out the credentials for the day.

Alas, the mother ship never landed.

The final theory I heard was that we were seeing a glint reflected from some international space station.

Funny how the mind works, eh?

Tell people what they want to hear and they'll happily buy into the lie. That was pretty much how the show brainwashed the contestants, after all...

BREAKING AND EXITING SIMON'S HOUSE

My first real interaction with Simon was an odd one. Everyone knew he had a massive stake in the show, not the least because of the fact that his record company signed the winner of each show. He also fronted the money to cover recording costs and things like that.

In truth, he was only part of the situation for a few seconds but that didn't make it any less odd.

Back when I was a Production Assistant and basically just dipping my toe in before getting my feet properly wet with Idol, I was stopped by a producer and asked if I was free to run an errand. That was pretty much my job, and I was free, but I needed to piss like a racehorse, so I told her I would meet her in her office when I was done. There's nothing particularly unique about toilets anywhere in the world. They serve a function, and function served you zip up. So, function served and zipped up, I washed my hands and made my way to her office.

I was told that Nigel and Ken had just signed off on the final cut of the last audition episode and it needed to be hand delivered to Simon's house before he hopped on a plane and headed back over the pond to his home country. A big deal was made about the 'hand delivery'. I took the tape, and checked in with the Adderall-and-porn loving production coordinator to let him know where I was going.

I had made maps to all the judge's and Ryan's homes and kept the copies in the glove box of my Explorer because I was always running to and from their houses delivering everything from clothing to scripts—the scripts covered everything from the stage movements to dialogue, who wears what, what song they sing. It is all meticulously planned out.

I jumped into my Explorer, gunned the engine and made my around the parking lot, turning onto Beverly Boulevard. It sounds glamorous, the sun in my eyes, wind in my hair, I headed toward Beverly Hills. The truth was I had had minimal interaction with Simon, and long before I hit La Cienega I realized that I had never actually been out to his house. The standard operating procedure when things needed to be delivered to him was to fire them off by messenger. Apparently there weren't any available today, or with him jumping on a plane the time frame for a messenger wouldn't make the cut. I let my imagination run wild, picturing his house as a fortress surrounded by high walls and heavy security....and as the cherry on top I added a couple of snipers sitting in trees to the mental image. I made a right turn onto La Cienega and proceeded up the street until it turned into Sunset Boulevard.

I veered off Sunset before it turned into the residential area of Beverly Hills where the massive multi-story office buildings end. I'm not sure if he owned the house I was heading to, or if he was just renting it, but it was a nice piece of real estate on Loma Vista Drive.

Or I assumed it was. I couldn't find it.

After driving up and down the street like some John crawling the curb looking for a trick, I came up empty. So I pulled over and called the office. Someone would know which house was his, or so I thought. But again I struck out. I wasn't feeling particularly lucky, but thankfully Clint wasn't around to ask me how I was doing. So, the next best thing, I figured, was to just go door-to-door… well, intercom-to-intercom. Of course I felt like an idiot, but it was part of my job and in my head was the producer's voice making a big deal about how the tape had to be in his hand before he took off for the airport. I started at the bottom of the street and pushed the intercom button, waited for the hired help to answer (the filthy rich don't answer intercoms, it's against their social code), and introduced myself, told them what show I was from and told them I had a tape to deliver. After going through half a dozen houses or so I finally found the right one, and boy was I right in assuming it would resemble a fucking fortress.

A twelve-foot tall solid beige brick colored wall and a matching twelve-foot tall black security gate that blocked any view from the driveway surrounded the entire property. I could also see security cameras every twelve feet or so. He liked his twelves. I guess it is some sort of mystical number where he comes from. I informed the butler who I was and what I was delivering. I was immediately told that I was not allowed to drive up the drive way, and that I had to park on the street making sure not to block the intercom, and walk up to the front door.

I mean, seriously?

My car had 4 wheels and ran on gasoline just like his. I hadn't been in an accident since I moved to LA so my driving skills had obviously improved and I wasn't stoned yet—but like the good Hollywood player I was, I knew I would be by the end of the scene, literally or metaphorically—so what was the problem?

I bit the bullet and did as I was told. I parked on the street, but just to be an asshole and specifically because I had been told not to do it I blocked the intercom.

It was a little bit of petty revenge that made me feel better for the rest of the day.

As soon as I opened my door the gate started to open – it didn't grind, it was well oiled, another metaphor in there, I am sure — so I grabbed the tape and hustled up the driveway, followed by all the security cameras. I checked the date. It wasn't 1984.

The driveway was steep (as the house sat above and behind the others on Loma Vista) and longer than I would have liked, given the heat. It curved slightly to the left until it opened up to a courtyard with an ugly-ass fountain right in the middle.

It was the kind of centerpiece that begged the question: 'Why are rich people so god damn tacky?' I'll never get that, not until my dying day, I swear. Ugly marble statues, gold leaf everywhere, ugly fountains. Unless your name is Nelson how many lion statues do you really need in your front yard?

One good lion statue would probably feed a small third world country for a month. Okay, I digress. BCSD's (big flashy expensive cars, I'll let you work the acronym out for yourself, but it is something about small penises) have never done anything for me, but I really had no choice but to look at them as the driveway was packed full of them. Now I freely admit I don't know my Volvos from my Mercedes, but I saw two Rolls Royce's (one black and one royal blue), one Ferrari (red, I think), and a silver Bentley Continental. It was like walking through a Ludicrously Expensive Car Graveyard; impressive to the ivory hunter, not so much to me. I weaved in and out of the cars and passed by the marble lion statues as I made my way towards the front door. Lurch had already taken up position and was waiting with a "you are wasting my time, mortal," look on his face.

The butler and I did not exactly hit it off.

"Yes," Butler said.

"I am here to deliver this," I responded, holding out the package and imaging it was actually carefully wrapped anthrax. I wasn't about to hand it over until it was in the right man's hands.

"Well you can just give it to me," Butler said. "I will make sure he gets it," Butler's white glove reached out in my direction.

"No, no, no. See I was told I needed to hand deliver it to him before he jumps on the plane." I explained, not quite reasonably.

"Now, listen here, young man, you can just give it to me," and then like something out of a BBC Regency Bonnet Production, he said, "We are far too busy to be bothered by petty requests. I will take the tape. Thank you." It was delivered with an imperiousness that just got my back up.

"What part of no don't you understand? Hand delivered means put into his hand. I wasn't told to give it Jeeves. I was told to give it to him directly. To place it in his hand. I am just doing my job."

Butler was getting riled. I could read it all over his red face. I couldn't help but enjoy it a little bit. Another petty revenge. After going back and forth for another couple of minutes and Butler's head turning almost puce and threatening to explode, he finally gave in. There was no legitimate reason that Simon couldn't come to the door, take the tape from my hand, blow a big ass lungful of smoke in my face, not thank me for anything, and then slam the door while I was still coughing. Butler said he would be back and closed the door, while I stood there waiting for them to return. I had plenty of time to send a text message back to my partner in crime at the office filling her in on more of the Trials and Tribulations of Justin Buckles, PA. Text sent, I had nothing else to do so I started taking pictures of the gaudy lions and fancy cars with my camera phone. Everyone's Paparazzo in Tinsel Town. A few choice shots of Chez Judge would of come in handy down the road if I ever wanted to sell my story to a tabloid magazine.

The door suddenly flew open and standing there in front of me was Mr. Cowell himself. Our five-second interaction was taking place.

"You have something for me?" He asked.

"Sure do," I said. "Final audition tape from the office." I handed it to him.

"Thank you. You can see yourself out." He took the tape from me and disappeared behind the door.

That was it.

Butler stood there staring at me with a look of disgust on his face. It didn't bother me in the slightest. I just gave him my best "fuck you" smile and walked away before he had the chance to slam the door in my face. Ah, petty victory number three. Petty victories really are underrated.

As I was making my way down the driveway I took out my cell phone and started taking a few more happy snaps of the property. I didn't really have a game plan for the pictures so I just snapped away randomly.

As I approached Hell's Gate – and it really did resemble that dread portal in a way, jet black and ominous – I figured that it would open on its own, tripped by some sort of sensor, and I would be able to walk right out. Of course, that would have been far too easy. I stopped within an arm's length of the gate, looked around, shrugged and started to jump up and down, hoping to set off either an underground sensor or some above-ground one. I wasn't really bothered as long as the gate opened. Of course, it didn't.

It didn't take Einstein's IQ to figure out I was officially locked inside the multimillion-dollar fortress of one of the wealthiest and most well known men on television. One thing was for certain, this was going to make an awesome story for the office, if I didn't starve to death here before I could share it. I scanned the ground on either side of the driveway looking for something that looked gate-related. Before I finished my scanning I realized that all the security cameras were following my every move. I was clearly being watched and figured that Butler was just being an asshole.

I stood up and extended both middle fingers as high into the air as possible and just for good measure made a complete circle so every single camera would get a money shot. I knew I was on my own at this point and there was no way I could go back to the front door and ask Butler for help, so after completing my full "fuck you" circle I had to think of a game plan. I have to admit I was loving every second of it. Give me a motorcycle and I could have been Steve McQueen in The Great Escape. How many people will ever get the chance to say they were basically held hostage by the most famous man on television? Without ever seeing it, I knew that I had the biggest shit-eating grin on my face. So, after living it up for a few minutes and snapping a few more pictures the penny finally dropped and I realized that yes, I was in fact trapped, and no one was coming to help me.

And if I called 911 what was I going to say?

"911 What's your emergency?"

"Well. Hmm. I'm not really sure if this qualifies as an emergency, given the fact that any given somewhere in Los

Angeles County right now I am sure there are drive-bys, rapes, gangbangs (and not the good sort, but some of those, too, probably, it was LA after all), murders and all that jazz going down, but I am trapped inside the Beverly Hills compound of the biggest asshole on television. Oh, and Hell's Gate is twelve foot tall so I can't scale it and make a run for it."

I am sure the call would be played back for the office Christmas party.

Out of my growing frustration, I ran toward the gate as fast as I could and threw myself bodily against it. I'm not sure what I was thinking, if I was thinking, maybe it would trigger something and the gate would miraculously open, because that's what happens when you assault security gates, right? Wrong. Being Steve McQueen wasn't as easily as it looked in the movies. All I had to show for my first escape attempt was a giant bruise on my left shoulder and arm when I woke up the next morning.

Nothing was happening with the gate. Butler was just rolling on the ground laughing at me, I knew, vindictive bastard that he obviously was. I ran over and tried to lift one the many marble statues that lined the driveway, knowing full well I wouldn't even be able to budge it, never mind hurl it against the gate.

In true War Movie fashion, the only thing left to do was to go over the top, though I was beginning to feel more like a chimp trying to escape my zoo than a '60s movie icon. I've been told I resemble a spider monkey a handful of times in my life, and now I come to think of it, I was actually was bitten by one right on the ass when, 6 years old, I visited a traveling petting zoo with my folks, so maybe I'd get lucky and discover a latent climbing Super Power like Spidey?

I scanned the area around me. To the right there was a large tree with a branch that, from where I stood, appeared to hang close to the wall, if not actually overhang it. I made my way through the nice, and I am sure ludicrously expensive, landscaping, doing my level best to step on each and every plant and flower that I could until I reached the tree. I did a few circles around the tree, looking for the lowest branch to pull myself up and, with luck, haul myself over the wall with. I made sure my phone and keys were secured in my pockets then grabbed the lowest branch with both hands and pulled myself up off the ground, swinging until I could wrap both of my legs around the branch. Just to complete the visual, I was hanging upside down like a possum. There was something almost perverse about the situation, and I am sure Alanis Morrisette would have said it was ironic: most people fantasize about breaking into multimillion-dollar celebrity homes in Beverly Hills, but there I was, hanging upside down busting my ass to break out of one.

I pulled myself up onto the branch and slowly started to stand up, using the trunk of the tree to stop me from falling. I got my balance. Whatever little devil looked after guys trying to break out of Celeb Mansions was doing a stand-up job. The branch did hang out over the wall. Baby step after baby step I edged towards my destination branch.

All that remained was for me to inch my way to the end of the branch and throw myself over the wall to freedom.

Easy.

Using a small upper branch for balance, I guided myself over to the ledge. I was at least twelve feet off the ground, given that the wall had to be every bit as high as Hell's Gate. Twelve feet is a long way down when you really don't feel like jumping. Far enough to hurt. I clung on to this little itsy bitsy branch and leaned out over the wall to see where I would actually be landing. Landing makes it sound graceful. Obviously I was looking for where I would fall. There was no grace about it. And, despite everything, that giant shit-eating grin returned. On the other side of the wall was more of that lush beautiful and ridiculously expensive landscaping, and in a few seconds I would be 'landing' right in the middle of it. No boulders, no rocks, no logs, no cars, and no people, just really expensive landscaping. I counted to three, made myself big, and jumped.

The shrubs swallowed me as I disappeared beneath them. I laid there for a second or two just to make sure that anyone in the area had just enough time to ignore the situation and move on. It was Beverly Hills after all. Once I realized I wasn't hurt, I stood up, shook off like a wet dog, and plucked at the branches and leaves that had tangled in my hair as I made my way back to my explorer.

So, unlike Steve McQueen, I made it out of the movie as a survivor. That's a good way of looking at it. Butler could just as easily have killed me and buried me at the bottom of the garden beneath one of the ludicrously expensive rose bushes, Simon could have had me fired, or you know, I could have broken my neck during the whole leap for freedom bit.

Of course, I had my suspicions throughout the rest of my time with the show that Simon not only knew what happened, but had been watching right along with Butler. There was something in the way he would smile at me.

That and he always said thank you for the smallest things.
No one else did.

FOX EXECUTIVES

Spend enough time around people and you start to get to know them whether you like it or not. You might never become best friends, but friendship in Hollywood is a pretty superficial thing anyway, so it isn't like you're missing out on anything.

I became familiar—that's a good word for it—with several of the Fox executives, including Mike Darnell, Tom Sheets, and Wenda Fond. I'd seen all of them during the Season 2 auditions, of course, but didn't have a clue who they were back then, outside of being the Big Wigs. The Honchos. Wenda and I were in regular contact because she was my go-to person at Fox whenever they wanted to put someone on the credentials list. We probably exchanged a dozen or so emails a week. Some Thursdays I'd have to deliver the show tickets to the Fox lot. I'd take them directly to Wenda who then had her assistants count them while I sat just outside of her office and waited.

I've got to admit I enjoyed seeing Wenda whenever I got the chance. She's genuine. There aren't many genuine people in TV. She was incredibly nice every time I saw her. She went out of her way to call me by name – hell she *remembered* my name, which was above and beyond the call for most of the others – and always asked how my day was going and how I was doing. It's just common courtesy in the real world but there's nothing common about it in TV.

She was a knockout. We're talking drop dead, smoking, gorgeous, a babe, a fox, a Fox fox, so to speak. Always dressed to the nines, understood color and how to coordinate without a style guru to hold her hand, and had manners. Manners go a long way.

During the beginning of Season 3 she asked me for my home address because she wanted to send me a few things that she thought I ought to have, but rather than ship them over to the office she preferred sending them somewhere she knew I'd get them. That said a lot about the show in itself. A few days later a bunch of stuff arrived in the mail: show posters, visors, glasses, t-shirts, you name it, all of the merchandize associated with the show. She didn't have to do this, but she understood that a little kindness, just taking a few minutes out of the day to show you appreciate someone, went a long way.

She was a breath of fresh air in the Santa Ana winds sweeping through the Los Angeles basin. She took the time out of her day to notice what was going on around her, and appreciate the 'little people' on the show. Even now, I couldn't think more highly Wenda. She was a class act. She treated everyone equally regardless of rank or title, which, if you ask me, is exactly how you should do the job.

Tom Sheets, on the other hand, had more in common with a lump of coal than any of the more evolved carbon-based lifeforms. I never heard him say more than ten words, and those weren't strung together into actual honest to God sentences. He obviously bought a defective personality when he went shopping for his. He never so much as looked at me, never mind said an actual word, even when I was in charge of credentials and we were supposed to interact. He would take his from my proffered hand and that would be that. No thank you, nothing. Nada. Zip. Zilch. Mind you, that wasn't such a hardship, the guy was a prescription-free cure for Insomnia.

Mike Darnell, Mike, Mike, Mike... what to say about Mike? If clothes maketh the man, Mike was a fringe-jacket-skin-tight-jeans-and-cowboy-boot wearing leprechaun. That's a not so subtle way of saying he could have passed for a child actor as he bounced around the office. He was constantly on the move, constantly laughing, and lived with a permanent grin slapped across his face. Alas, for all that you'd want this bundle of energy to be a half-way decent human being he was one of mooks who never took the time to develop a shred of decency when it came to the rank and file. When I think about Mike, one thing sticks out in my mind throbbing red and angry like a sore thumb: he had to have a box of Honey Nut O's cereal. Couldn't live with out it. The stuff was his crack. He was forever checking in with the shows craft service person to make sure she had his fix. She didn't dare leave it on the table for fear that some unsuspecting fool would scoff the damned stuff and bring on O'smageddon. He'd carry his box of O's with him wherever he went, munching straight out of the box, going elbow deep by the time we were ready to air. Mike was quite possible the oddest leprechaun I ran across during my entire time in Hollywood.

ISOLATION

Another constant gripe amongst the contestants and their guardians was the isolation. They had no contact with the outside world. They were forced to pull their Myspace and Facebook profiles and take down all of those other social networking websites that had started to spring up all over the Internet. They had to nix any pictures of themselves that they had posted on the Internet and anything else that pertained to them. Patrick McGoohan's Prisoner might have been a name, not a number, but the contestants weren't even that.

By this stage of things they were expected to be utterly anonymous and completely show-owned.

The show preferred it this way. They wanted total control of the contestants' images and accompanying image rights, meaning they got to exploit those images in whatever way promised to make the show the most money. Too many other pictures out there diluted this potentially lucrative avenue as far as they were concerned.

Be careful what you wish for, right? And hell, be careful what you sign your name to. It didn't take long for most of the contestants to start questioning what it was they'd actually signed when they'd done their deal with the Devil, but of course the fine print was never thoroughly explained to them. And it was inevitable that Shylock would want his pound of flesh sooner or later. One contestant told me that not only had nothing about the contents of their contract ever been explained, that the inference was, "if you want to be part of the show you sign this now, otherwise bye bye," which, given everything else I know about Idol, I can well believe.

It wasn't as though the lines of communication were open for the contestants or guardians to actually ask about certain odious clauses in their contracts. Even though they were in the process of becoming household names I couldn't help but feel sorry for them. It was like the old intro to Fame: Fame costs and right here's where you start paying.

Look, there's no point in me pretending what I think. It's pretty obvious from everything else I've said so far, but just in case you're in any doubt, right here, right now let me say I believe, hand on heart, Idol is a business, and as a business doesn't give a shit about *nurturing* the talent, it's all about *exploiting* the talent. Everything about the show is designed to take advantage of the contestants in order to generate money for the show. That's the cold hard truth. It isn't about caring for these kids that are being thrown out to the wolves. They aren't even kids, they're dollar signs plain and simple. The producers and execs are scheming away like Dick Dastardly behind the scenes to come up with new schemes that prostitute the contests for the All Mighty Dollar.

It's all about maximizing the season's revenue.

Don't look so surprised, you didn't think they did this out of any sense of altruism or debt to the world of 'art' did you? Nah, didn't think so.

Money, Money, Money, as Abba's relentless '70s pop jingle says.

There were plenty of reminders about just what was important over the course of any given season, but none more so than during a show day when the *American Juniors* winners arrived to attend the taping.

I'd grown particularly close to one of the mothers during the season. We'd developed a big sister/little brother thing. So I was absolutely thrilled to see her. I had no idea the kids were attending. I walked over with this huge grin on my face, and as soon as I was close enough she just leaned in and said, "I've got so much to tell you," and shook her head in obvious disgust.

I still had a few things to do before I could sit down and chat properly with her, so I promised I'd finish up as quickly as I could and find my way back to her. I knew she had some dirt to dish, which was one reason to want to find her, but really I just wanted to spend a little time with my surrogate Big Sis. She gave me a huge hug when I got back and said, "Well, that's pretty much it."

It didn't make much sense as an opening gambit, so I asked her what she was meant.

Without going into too much detail she explained that almost immediately after the show ended the behind the scenes players, the production company and the management team, lost all interest in the group. As far as she was concerned they'd been spun one huge elaborate lie for the sole purpose of exploiting her child. There were no future plans for the group, no upcoming appearances, no nothing. They'd been on TV all summer and then it was as though they simply ceased to exist. It had become so bad they'd lost all interest in being part of the group. She'd made call after call after call trying to get someone on the phone so she could figure out what her child could and couldn't do based on the contract she'd signed because she wanted to take advantage of the fact that they had just spent the entire summer on television. But she could never get ahold of anyone. The only reason she was attending the taping of the show was because she was under contract to do so.

I told her I was glad she was there.

There was nothing else I could say.

THE TREATMENT OF THE CONTESTANTS

This sort of thing was typical of the show, and a damning reflection of society as a whole.

As soon as you were eliminated you're gone, forgotten about until the finale and the summer tour across America. And then when that is done, it's back to the pile of obscurity for you. It's like you've been cut out of all the family photos.

It is all fiscal at the end of the day. If management sees no new ways to make money off your hide what possible use are you to them?

But you know what's funny about being clipped out of the family photos when it comes to this particularly dysfunctional family? The show continues to exploit your images, recordings and appearance to generate millions of dollars a year while you make nothing.

Riddle me this, if the management team is that amazing and does such an outstanding job with the careers of the contestants why have so many of them "bought" themselves out of their contracts as soon as possible? If all was hunky dory in Idol Land and the contestants were being looked after and treated fairly why would they buy themselves out of their contract?

Hmm... "Curiouser and curiouser," cried Alice (she was so much surprised, that for the moment she quite forgot how to speak good English).

I am not saying that every contestant buys their way out, because obviously they don't. But as several former contestants have, then surely there's something rotten in the state of Idol. If you ask me, the contestants are treated much like the rest of the employees are. They're forced to work long arduous shifts, at times up to twenty hours a day, for minimal pay. They're exploited for financial gain and treated like slave labor.

This was one of the main reasons Brian Dunkleman, Season 1's co-host, didn't come back for the second season. He's made it abundantly clear through numerous interviews that he didn't like the way the contestants were treated.

And good for him, say I.

THE JUDGE'S DRESSING ROOMS

Another one of our duties involved cleaning the judge's dressing rooms after show day.

It was fairly painless. Most of the time they weren't particularly messy.

Paula's always smelled like cheap perfume and lotion.

Simon's, even after he got his smokeless ashtray, reeked of stale cigarette smoke. I never paid that much attention to Randy, so to be honest, I really don't recall what his dressing room smelled like during Season 3.

Then, last of the heap, was Ryan's. The guy regularly took showers in his dressing room after showing up at the studio fresh from a work out. I would say out of all the dressing rooms, his was, without fail, the messiest.

One reason not to complain about this duty was that the judges always left good 'material' lying around. We're talking notes and paperwork, great stuff to feed the gossip mill and keep the crew talking. I never found anything particularly incriminating, just notes jotted down during phone calls and meetings. But every now and again I'd come across something amusing.

One such find that turned up in both Ryan and Simon's dressing rooms were lifts that they inserted into their shoes to make themselves appear taller than they really were. Clothes and shoes were always tossed around the room. It wasn't their responsibility to put their wardrobe away. That was the show's stylist's job. Not that Simon had much of a wardrobe. He generally wore whatever he showed up in.

Ryan on the other hand had thousands of dollars worth of designer clothes in his dressing room at any given time, with several thousand dollars more in the wardrobe room on the third floor.

I tried his clothes on.

Most of them were pretty tacky, especially the T-shirts and undershirts that he wore.

I found these lifts every week. At least I assume they were lifts. They were both on the short side. Shorter, or maybe the same size as me, it was hard to tell for sure, but I am a not so towering 5'8". It's all part of the optical illusion of television, even short people can be made to look like tall people if you shoot it just so.

Ryan was always on his feet, and there were plenty of occasions he found himself standing beside one of the female contestants in their heels and the ladies towered over him. It can't have been easy being the little guy on the block, so yeah, I assume they were lifts.

FAN MAIL

Throughout the season fan mail came pouring into the office. We're talking sacks and sacks of the stuff on a daily basis.

The receptionist always collected this, but it was never distributed among the contestants or the judges. So if you're wondering why you never got that answer, now you know.

Fan mail was tossed in boxes that were kept under the reception desk.

On slow days we'd entertain ourselves by grabbing a box stuffed full with those earnest letters and open them. We'd read the best of them aloud and laugh our asses off at the fact that the writer had taken so much time and effort (and let's not forget spent money) to write and mail the letter with the reasonable assumption that it would eventually make it into the hands of the whoever they'd addressed it to.

We were jerks.

It was cruel and mean, but the sad reality is when your boss and the show's execs are all laughing along with you, you keep doing it. You're the performing monkey wanting to keep the organ grinder happy. It never hurts to get on the organ grinder's good side when you're his monkey.

If pictures were included in the fan mail we'd typically take them and deface them, drawing mustaches and other 'amusing' facial blemishes before putting them up on the bulletin board.

If they were from corporations or charities asking for something we'd typically scrunch them up and toss those straight into the recycle bin basketball-style.

If it was clothing, and we got sent lots of t-shirts and stuff, we'd see who they fit best and said donation would go to them.

If it was jewelry the female production assistants would fight over it.

I can remember Fantasia being sent Tevana Tea by a fan, a rather expensive gift that I shared with another employee during a late night in the office. We brewed up cups, liked it, and decided to split it between us.

It was wrong.

It's easy to say that now, but better to admit the fact that we did some appalling stuff than just try and make like we were all angels. People were spending a lot of money on some of these gifts, the whole family-orientated nature of the show making them think we'd all be honest and pass on their gifts. I wish I could say I can remember a single time one of the letters made it all the way to any of the contestants, but I can't. Not once.

It's unconscionable. What bothers me most about this is the fact that the vast majority of the fans sending these letters and gifts in were young kids. They sent the stuff in thinking that the pictures they colored, the art that they made, the letters that they hand wrote, the stuff they sent in hopefully for autographs, would get to their heroes, when in reality they wound up in the trash.

So what happened if they'd enclosed a self-addressed stamped return envelope with the goodie they hoped to have autographed? Surely they made it to the contestants for a signature, right? Wrong. One of the production assistants would sign it as best they could, usually a scribble and the word love or a heart, and drop in into the outgoing mailbox.

One guy sent in a stack of stuff to be signed by the judges that were going to be auctioned off for charity. They asked for signatures and they got them, only they weren't the judge's signatures.

I'd say if you bought anything that was supposed to have been signed by one of the judges it's highly unlikely it's authentic. There's a better chance that I signed it than Simon did.

Artists made pictures and paintings for the judges, they were all tossed in the trash when they arrived because they were too cumbersome to carry over from the mailroom. Back then we were receiving so much mail we had to trek over to the CBS mailroom to collect it ourselves because there was too much for the mailroom guys to deliver. Anything that big just wasn't worth dragging back.

The judges were inundated with gifts from companies hoping for a little free product placement or press in exchange. Lotions, creams, perfumes, beauty products, clothes, new food products, they could easily have gone a decade without having to pay for any of this stuff. Of course the judges never asked for any of this shit. So guess who got it? Yep, more swag for the show's crew. Hell, I sent my mom an entire tote bag full of products, which I know included several hundred dollars worth of products and perfumes. I took home my fair share of stuff too, body scrubs and toners, shampoos, gels, and everything in between.

It's not that we didn't want to give everything to the contestants and judges.

We were told we *couldn't*.

The contestants weren't allowed to have them for fear that it could possibly cause friction among them. Imagine one guy getting seven sacks of mail and the others getting one between them. Fan mail's a great way to judge popularity outside of the phone-in votes. And make no bones about it, Idol's all one big popularity contest when it comes down to it. Being underestimated can be every bit as powerful a weapon as being a firm favorite, don't forget.

As far as the judges and Ryan went, well they had ample money to buy all the shit their hearts could desire so what were a few freebies in the mail?

THE STAND-INS

I was in the office one Monday early on during Season 3 – I know it was fairly early in the season because the majority of the contestants were still standing – while the performance and elimination rehearsals were going on downstairs. The actual shows would take place over the next two days, but the script had to be run through, all the cues tested, the Idol machine put through its paces.

The rehearsals were done with stand-ins rather than the actual contestants.

Each stand-in wore a giant sticker on the front and back of their shirts so everyone knew who they were supposed to be.

These rehearsals took place so Nigel and Ken could map out the way they wanted the show to unfold step-by-step right up to the elimination of the contestant. Everything was choreographed, from where the contestants stood, to how they entered and exited the stage. Light tracking, camera tracking, it all had to be practiced so the show could go as smoothly as possible for the live send. No one wants to see a clusterfuck spinning around on stage.

As I sat at my desk, I was approached by a producer who wanted me to run a message downstairs to one of the other producers sitting in on the rehearsals.

I had nothing else to do so I said sure, thinking it would

be a simple run with the added bonus that I could raid the craft service table on the way. The table was always set up just outside the sound stage where the show taped so the camera, audio, and any other crew members could grab a snack before heading back to their duties. It was all about keeping time away from their posts down to a minimum of course, not about nutrition or welfare.

These rehearsals were closed door, which meant they were off-limits to the majority of staff. It was essential personnel only behind the door, so only the ones who had a part in how the show unfolded. Huge man-mountain security guards blocked both doors to the stage. The main stage door is massive, we're talking two stories tall and well on its way to being a foot thick. It's seriously heavy duty steel, which is needed to block out all the outside sound.

I knew there was no way I'd get in through the main doors, but tried anyway just to see if I was right. I approached the security guard and told him I had an urgent note for one of the producers inside, from another producer up in the office. I was told I would have to enter through the back entrance, just down from the green room, where the contestants typically entered. I headed to the door to find another security guy standing guard there.

I didn't understand what was so secretive that these rehearsals had to be closed door.

I mean the entire tension/suspense notion of the show was down to audience participation and the phone-in votes, everything else was just walk here, stand there, say boo, so why were security blocking access to the stage?

Was it really that important that the show stand-ins had complete privacy? It wasn't as though they were celebrities, after all.

So why all the hush-hush stuff unless there was stuff they really didn't want people seeing? And what could possibly be so devastating to the integrity of the show if people did see it?

It was a constant cause of speculation amongst the production assistants because we all had to get behind those closed doors at one time or other, either to deliver something or bring in lunch, or even just usual Starbucks orders of skinny lattes and low-fat mochas.

So I went through the whole explanation again when I reached the next security guard, what I'd been given, who had given it to me, and who needed get it. I impressed the urgency of it on him, twisting his arm until let me in. He told me to stay to the left of the stage and as close to the wall as possible, and basically said I needed to be a church mouse and make as little noise as possible. I was to stay in the shadows of the stage. I agreed, already knowing the drill. He was only doing his job so I listened, nodded and thanked him, then walked through the door as he held it open.

I stayed to the left of the stage, tripping on a pile of loose cables that had just been thrown on the floor instead of taped down. Who needed to worry about health and safety? Not Idol. Cables weren't taped down, signs weren't present where they needed to be. People fell on a regular basis both in front of and behind the stage, including Jabba at one point. Apparently she had no idea how the actual set was put together and didn't realize that it was built using transparent materials, so she mistook a step that wasn't there and went down in a pile of blubber before a close-to-full audience. The chaos that followed her prat-fall was a thing of beauty. She was rushed upstairs to her office and fussed over. A production assistant was told to fill up her ice machine. Her ice machine was basically a cooler that had a cuff attached that she would secure around her knees, and pump up, like she was taking her blood pressure. Her knees were in terrible shape from lugging all of that fat around, so she used this ice machine to circulate ice cold water around her knees to keep them from swelling as the day went on. Maybe it was Karma being a bitch. A little payback for the way she treated the employees? I'd like to think so. Heck, it's the kind of thought that would keep me warm and cozy at night.

Anyway, I digress.

I made my way around the stage. The producer I needed sat in the front row of chairs and seemed to be involved in a pretty heated discussion with another producer. It didn't take me long to realize they had different opinions on how the show should be unfolding. I loitered, doing my best to be invisible, waiting for their little spat to finish so I could sneak up behind my guy and slip him the note. It was like waiting for a drug deal to go down on the corner of Hollywood and Vine.

But it didn't take me long to realize this particular fight was going to last for a while, so I plopped my ass down in one of the chairs, and made sure my phone was off. The last thing I wanted was for someone to call, or a text to chime in because it'd be me against the world then. I didn't fancy the Tongue Lashing of a Thousand Cuts and the way these guys were getting cranked up there was nothing to say it wouldn't come to blows. It was getting to the point where violence had been bumped up from a last resort to a genuine way of resolve things in the office. It was worse than being back in the schoolyard. No one had the inter-personnel skills to just sit down and talk like a rational human being. Instead it was blood and thunder. The logic seemed to be scream loudly enough and you were bound to learn your lesson.

After what passed for healthy debate around there, the call was made again for all the stand-ins to take their place on the stage so they could go over everything one more time.

They all took their places as Nigel and Ken stood at the foot of the stage ordering them around like Khufu lashing his slaves for being too slow building his blessed Pyramid. I wasn't about to make my move now. The last thing I wanted to do was draw attention to myself, and the producer was so intently focused on what was happening on stage I knew he wouldn't thank me for interrupting, so I just sat there and watched. I had time on my hands and figured what the hell, if I had to sit in on this rehearsal until it was done then that's what I was going to do. I was playing it safe. Us lowly assistants weren't supposed to bother the producers until they were free to talk, and preferably not until they came and asked us for something. If they were in the middle of something interrupting them was *verboten*.

So, I sat back and watched an absolute train wreck of a rehearsal unfold before my eyes.

It wasn't as though they hadn't done this a million times before, but looked as though it was their first time and they were terrified of busting their cherry.

Of course, I didn't get to see this stuff week-in week-out, so maybe this was the way it was every week? You'd like to imagine that after a few years it'd be a well-oiled machine though, wouldn't you?

I watched them bring the final three stand-ins to the front of the 'middle stage' area, and one by one they were told if they were safe or not. Then they eliminated the stand-in contestant, signed off on how it was going to happen, and then called a wrap on the rehearsal.

I delivered my message and grabbed a handful of gummy

bears from the craft service table on the way out.

As Tuesday's show aired, we all gathered round to watch it in the holding area just outside the soundstage that was set up specifically for us. The production assistants set about the craft service table devouring just about every scrap of food that had been laid out. It was always the production assistants who suffered when it came to meal breaks and rest periods so they feasted like junk food kings when they had the chance.

Like every other week, as soon as the show ended and the lights came up, we all scattered like cockroaches and headed back to the office to wrap out the day. It was our one chance to get home at a decent hour.

When the results show rolled around on Wednesday we again assembled to watch it downstairs, again shoveling in as much sugar-rich junk food as our faces would hold. I didn't think anything of it at the time, but on the drive home it hit me: the stand-in I'd watched eliminated in rehearsal was the same contestant that had gone out during the results show.

Peculiar? Hell yes. You don't need me to tell you how much was at stake when it came to making sure the right people won. Think about it, the rehearsals took place before any of the voting had happened, and yet the same contestant went out on both occasions.

Look, it may have been a coincidence, I know that. Stranger things happen at sea and all that jazz. It was the only rehearsal I watched all the way to the wrap. It could have been a case of pure blind luck that the same contestant was eliminated. But you're familiar with Occam's Razor, right? The simplest explanation tends to be the correct one. If it looks like a turd and smells like a turd, it probably is a turd. When you factor in the sheer amount of money riding on recordings and all those sundry rights, I can't believe the people with so much invested in the success of the show would risk it essentially on the roll of the dice. These guys fixed song selections, manipulated rehearsal times with the vocal coaches, and did everything else in their power to make sure the right ones went through, so with all that knowledge tucked away in the back of my mind I couldn't see how it could have fallen so neatly into place the way that it had if it wasn't all pre-planned and went along with the final script approved by the likes Nigel and Ken.

If nothing else, it makes you wonder...

FLIPPING A COIN

What I can't do is say for sure and certain it was rigged.

I never saw another rehearsal so I don't know if every other week the eliminations didn't match up. I know they have to eliminate a person every week, that's the nature of the game after all, and I know they have to rehearse, because all of the technicians and light guys and audio guys need to nail their cues, and I know if you toss a coin one hundred times in a row it's conceivable it could turn up heads every time, but it's unlikely. So I'm left to wonder if the show's as genuine as it portrays itself.

I mean, do the votes count at all?

Is it all known and worked out in advance?

Here's what I will say: I honestly think that decisions on the show pertaining to the contestants and eliminations are not fully controlled by the voting public, but rather the executives have the final say so in who goes and who stays.

Of course they want you to believe otherwise.

They're selling you a rags to riches dream, after all. Who wants to believe Cinderella's been picked out by anything other than the glass slipper?

A HOP, SKIP AND A JUMP

If you think about it, it makes perfect sense that insiders would have control over the contestants, the eliminations, and how the drama all unfolds.

Sure, the judges clearly can sway the public with some carefully chosen words, or not so carefully thought out treatment in those few moments after the performance. It doesn't stretch the imagination too much to figure out if they're showing favoritism towards a certain contestant that will inevitably rub off on the viewers. It's a hop, skip and a jump to them reciprocating and showing the same sort of favoritism towards the same contestant.

People are fairly easily manipulated.

If I can make them stare at aliens in the sky, I think that the judges are more than capable of swaying the publics opinion, don't you?

FANTASIA

As the season rolled on, contestant after contestant eliminated, the standout, far and away public favorite was Fantasia. She was fantastic, had a hell of a set of lungs on her, and everyone loved her. She was, perhaps, a little naïve in that she never seemed to know what was going on around her, only that she was there to sing. It was rather endearing, really. She loved to talk about her daughter, and it was obvious she loved her dearly and missed her every single minute when she wasn't around, which was most of the time. She would come into town with the rest of her family to attend a taping of the show, but that was it.

There was always plenty of talk amongst the employees—from production assistants all the way up to the executives—that they did not want Diana to win because no one wanted to have to deal with her mother.

Daylight Savings Time?

On the day of the finale I was the first to arrive at the Kodak Theater, bright-eyed and bushy tailed at 4 in the morning.

It was deserted. Not so much as a lingering Dark Knight to be seen. I was told the production office would be unlocked and opened, and there'd be a security guard making sure that no one entered without the full authenticated credential passes that we'd all been wearing during the finale week, as well as our usual badges from CBS.

I held up my end of the stick, and arrived as promised at 4 in the morning, meaning I'd dragged myself out of bed at 2:30, managed a few pushups, and half-drowned myself under a blazing hot shower. But I really didn't want to wake up. I shuffled zombie-like into the Kodak Theater and shambled right up to the security booth, all set to show my credentials and security badges, not that there was anyone in the security booth when I arrived.

It had always been expecting too much for the other end of the stick to be held up.

I wandered around a bit looking for any signs of life.
Nothing.
I went back to the double doors and gave them a try. Surprise, surprise, they were unlocked as well as unguarded.

Nice, considering there was millions of dollars worth of equipment and supplies inside. So I moseyed on back to the production office hoping to find the missing security guard, but of course he was nowhere to be found.

So what else was I supposed to do besides start making my way through the maze surrounding the theater?

I swear I went in a few circles. I was still half-asleep and in dire need of that first a cup of java, which was supposed to be brewing around 5 in the morning. I was counting down the minutes. Twenty of them were wasted searching the theater for any signs of life. There wasn't a single person in place but everything was unlocked, all the dressing rooms, the holding areas, everywhere apart from the production office, which of course was where I needed to be.

So I resigned myself to sitting and waiting. I took off my backpack and leaned against the production office door. Needless to say I quickly fell asleep only to shoot bolt upright, wide awake, two minutes later. I had no idea what had woken me. It was as much as I could do to work out there were still thirty minutes until I could get my hands on coffee.

I started sending text messages to other staff members, including the head production assistant who told me to be there at 4 in the morning.

I got no response back. Let's face it; they were all fast asleep.

So I decided to throw the backpack on and do a quick recce around the mall area in the hopes of finding someone to let me into the office.

Of course, when I did, he had no idea what the hell was going on.

I tried to explain to him over and over who I was and what I was doing there. I showed him my credentials half a dozen times in five minutes, but none of it worked. His sage advice? Wait until the main security guard showed up in half an hour.

Yep, no one else was going to be there until 5.

So why the hell was it so important I was there at 4?

I wish I could say this was case of the left hand not knowing what the right hand was doing was a rarity, but it was fairly fucking common to be honest. The whole lack of communication was unlike anything I'd experienced before. No one knew what had or hadn't been done. No one ever followed-up to confirm stuff. So people doubled and tripled-up on projects. More than once I was sent out to run errands around Los Angeles, just grunt work like picking something up, only to arrive at the location and be told that said items had already been collected or delivered to the office already. Not that I minded. Sometimes it was just nice to get out, and I used my own car whenever I was running errands because we were reimbursed for mileage based on the current gas prices.

And sure, like everyone else, I lied on my reimbursement mileage forms. I'd doubled the miles that I actually drove. It wasn't like anyone ever checked up on them, so it was one way to get back some of the money they were stealing from me.

I'd fill out my mileage form every Friday, but being clever, I'd use a bunch of different colored pens to make it look like I'd filled it out after returning from the errands. No one ever monitored who was doing what, or where they were going. All that mattered was that the forms were complete. So it was one way to claw back a hundred or so bucks a week, which is what we in the trade call a Gift Horse.

The unspoken rule was if no one was going to monitor

anything you did, why not take advantage of that freedom? The same logic undermined every aspect of life behind the scenes, whether it was the spliffs in the parking lot or the miles on the odometer. The whole thing about being an unspoken rule, by definition, meant no one talked about it. Everybody knew it. Everybody did it. They just didn't talk about it.

REALITY IN THE TRASHCAN

Finally the security guard arrived.

I had to go through the whole who I was, what I was doing, palaver, showing him my credentials and security badge, before convincing him that I was allowed to be on site. I finally got into the production office and set about my duties, which included walking about the theater, taking down the schedules from the day before and replacing them with the new ones for the day. Then it was a case of making sure the coffee was up and running and that the craft service area was all set.

Since we were in the Kodak Theater we had to utilize their food services set up, which paled in comparison with the craft service areas back at CBS.

One of my other duties was to unlock the room where the senior, supervising, and executive producers could have their meetings. I needed to clean this area up from the day before and make sure it was stocked with bottles of water and a handful of snacks.

I took the opportunity to snoop around in the trash and see what I could find.

Yeah, yeah, yeah, we're talking about crumpled up notes, pieces of paper, an empty water bottle or two, and the odd few gum wrappers. Nothing icky. The vast majority of what I found were notes taken on the show's script. Last minute rewrites for Ryan, suggestions on what should and shouldn't be discussed. It was, after all, the biggest day of the year as far as the show was concerned, so it had to be very carefully crafted, this 'reality' they were peddling.

This didn't really surprise me in the slightest.

By now very little did.

ONE MAN, ONE VOTE

As the finale progressed, there was a lot of talk about what would happen with Diana's mom if Diana were to lose out to Fantasia. We took it seriously. I was told that I needed to keep an eye out for her, and if she was anywhere she wasn't supposed to be, I was to call security over the walkie-talkie and stay with her until they showed up.

Under no circumstances was she to be trusted at this point in proceedings.

It could all have been an elaborate joke, of course, I mean, if I enjoyed having hapless co-workers staring up at an empty sky looking for spacemen, who's to say someone else's idea of fun wasn't having us gullible plebs walking around jumping at Mommy Dearest-shaped shadows?

When the phone lines opened on the voting night of the finale we all picked up the land-lines that were installed in the production office and started placing calls for Fantasia again and again. People had their cellphones out too, double-teaming the vote counter.

Producers were running into the office grabbing the phones and making calls. Management from 19 Entertainment were in the room as well, and their fingers were doing the talking for them.

Ironically, I was always under the impression that we weren't allowed to vote because we worked on the show. But we must have placed hundreds – thousands – of votes between us. I can't recall with any great certainty, but I am pretty sure we waived our right to vote on the paperwork that we signed at the beginning of each season.

Considering we weren't allowed to have anything to do with them, I can't imagine we were supposed to be voting for them, can you?

Heck, I'd never seen a single employee vote before but it seemed like this was a special occasion. I went along with what everyone else was doing, voting my little heart out and making sure I was seen to be doing it because I was ready to grease whatever wheels needed to be greased for me to secure a position on the new season.

I spent a good thirty minutes hitting last number redial and calling in for Fantasia along with everyone else.

We laughed our asses off as we were doing it, hoping like hell our votes counted. We were united, a band of brothers in the trenches, doing our best to get Fantasia crowned the winner. It was just a bonus that the show was being charged every time we hit redial.

EARLY WARNING ELIMINATIONS

Nigel was doing the Ali-shuffle when he came into the production office the next morning. You know the one, floating like a butterfly. It was all over bar the shouting, so he didn't need to worry about stinging like a bee.

The way I understand it, the executive producers knew who was eliminated within a few seconds of the voting ending.

He made his way to the middle of the room and stood there looking around slowly, taking his time to be sure he had everyone's attention, and then he asked, "So, how many votes do you guys reckon came in last night? Go on, guess."

Sixty million's the number I remember. Apparently broke some sort of record. I'm pretty sure we responsible for more than our fair share.

A MOM ON FIRE

We were told again to keep an eye on Diana's mom.

The clock ticked on, the second hand edging us closer and closer to the results. It was surprisingly tense around the place. We were all wound up. Fantasia and Diana were both on stage with Ryan standing between them. I imagine he had his lifts in to give him that precious extra inch.

Obviously Fantasia won. It's ancient history in TV terms now.

I felt a momentary pang of guilt, not because of Fantasia's triumph, but well, hell, we didn't know how close the votes were or weren't. We had no way of knowing if our mad redials had really cost Diana the win. And for that moment, that pang, I felt a little sorry for her. But at least she never knew the entire office and all of the back room staff were frantically voting against her.

Diana's mom didn't take it well.

I didn't see it first hand, but I heard about it soon enough down the grapevine. Chinese whispers and all that. She probably stood up and shook her head, but by the time the story got back to me the second the cameras went dark Diana's mom launched herself out of her seat and stormed back stage. She was on fire and looking to burn any and all producers stupid enough to get too close to her naked flame.

The story went something like this: she yelled and screamed and was tackled by security, who restrained her with those plastic ties the police use, and after she'd burned herself out, she split leaving Diana alone when she really could have used a friend.

AND THAT'S A WRAP

As Season 3 came to a close we were dead on our feet and barely able to keep our eyes open after a fifteen hour day – seventeen in my case because of that whole 4 in the morning debacle – I jumped in my car and started to head home.

My life very nearly wrapped just as quickly as the season. I was driving along Laurel Canyon Road, one of the most treacherous roads in Los Angeles, (it's all tight curves and switchbacks, if you don't know it) when my eyelids started to droop and my head went down.

My head snapped up with barely a few feet between me and back of a car that was parked on the side of the road.

I swerved violently into the oncoming lane, really not the smartest thing to do in the circumstances, but thank fuck there were no oncoming cars. My heart raced. My eyes were wide, like PCP-wide, and sweat poured from every inch of my skin. It was *that* close. A matter of feet. Given the speed I was going, if I'd hit that car I would have been a goner. I knew it. And because I knew it, I started having a panic attack. I had to pull over to the side of the road. I rolled all the windows down and stuck my head out, gasping for air and trying to swallow as much oxygen as I could. I needed to calm down so I'd be able to drive the rest of the way home.

After what seemed like forever, but was probably only

about ten minutes, I felt okay enough to start the engine and drive home.

I keep all the windows rolled down and turned KROQ all the way up to eleven. I don't remember what the songs were, just that I played them loudly enough to make Spinal Tap proud.

I could see myself in the rearview mirror. I looked as if I'd snorted an entire eight ball of cocaine, my eyes were that wide and I looked that whacked out. I was absolutely fucking terrified of every twist and turn of the road that came. All I could think was that I had to stay awake. I couldn't blink. Not even for a second. God alone knows how, but I made it home in one piece.

That night, as I lay there in bed unable to sleep for the adrenalin still pumping through my system, I knew I'd come a little too close to meeting my maker for comfort, and all for some dumb television show.

Talk about a sobering moment.

But what do you expect when people are forced to work such ridiculously long hours again and again with next to no turnaround time before starting the next fifteen hour shift?

And it didn't help that I kept remembering the camera man who lost his life while making his way home, same as me, after too many days in a row, with too little downtime to rest and recharge. He died for his job. I came that close, and it freaked me out.

I couldn't sleep at all that night. I tossed. I turned. The few seconds that my guard slipped and I went down, I slipped into a nightmare and panicked myself back awake.

It wasn't a good night.

NO, REALLY, THAT'S A WRAP

The following morning I was a mess.

It must have been bad because people actually noticed.

They asked me several times if I was okay. I told them the truth: that I fell asleep on the drive home and woke up within feet of slamming into the back of a parked car.

They were all heart.

They called me a pussy and laughed. These, ladies and gentlemen, were the fine people I was working with. It was a bit of an eye-opener. Maybe it was black humor in the face of reaper, or maybe they were just pricks. I'll let you decide.

And that's how I ended Season 3, and how Season 3 came so, so close to ending me.

SECURING WORK ON SEASON 4

Contrary to the movie-line there are very few happy endings in Hollywood.

Everyone might write about mythic structure and the hero's journey, but it isn't as if normal folks like us are even the heroes of our own lives most of the time, so how are we supposed to be Hollywood heroes? We end up tending bar or waiting tables at Mel's Diner and pretending it's still the set of *American Graffiti*. You'll find us delivering pizzas and serving lattes, skinny, double shot, tall, non-dairy blah blah blah with cinnamon sprinkles on top. Don't forget the sprinkles.

What I'm trying in my not so subtle way to say is that there was no job security for the crew, at least not those at the bottom of the totem pole.

Me, I had no idea what lay in store for me after the finale.

I could have been out on my ear the next day.

As it was, I was asked to stay on and help break everything down and close out of the theater. I was one of the Wizard's helpers, getting to see the illusions of Oz stripped down to nothing. That made me one of the lucky ones. Most of the production assistants were told not to come back, any question about their future answered with the charming, "If you hear from us, you hear from us," if they were lucky enough and someone somewhere deigned to answer. The rest were ignored.

Since I was asked to do the take down I figured I had to have a foot in the door for Season 4. So I did what I did best. I put on a happy face and did everything that was asked of me, and hoped it'd lead to me being part of the production office on a permanent basis.

Idol is a rolling show, basically it's like the song that never ends, you know the one? I know a song that'll get on your nerves, get on your nerves, get on your nerves, this is a song that'll get on your nerves.... or my personal favorite, you remind me of a man, what man? A man with power. What power? The power of hoodoo. Who do? You do. What? Remind me of a man.... what man? repeat into nauseum. Months before the finale for Season 3 is even a blip on the radar, back-room staff are already prepping for the Season 4 audition tour. Producers and members of the security team are flying out to look at venues and cities for a couple days at a time, more often than not on Thursday's and Friday's because they're down days and they wouldn't have to miss any of the live shows.

I figured I had a decent chance of being asked to tag along as the circus traveled around the country, but at the same time I knew the show already had a production coordinator and head production assistant, both higher up the chain than I was, so after a couple of weeks bumming around the office I decided I'd skip out for week and booked a flight home to Coos Bay.

A Son in TV

It was always great to go home, and with my father's health declining I knew there wouldn't be many more real trips home. Home, you see, isn't the walls or the cliffs and woods or the winding paths and the dirt tracks and the ballparks where you pitched and struck out as a kid, it isn't the ghosts you see in every shop window you walk by along the high street, the first girl you kissed, the first, first, first, none of that, though they all come together to make the place special. Home is where your family is, mum, dad, brothers, sisters, and soon mine would be diminished forever, so this time when I went home I was determined to savor each and every minute. No stupid sibling squabbles, no grumbles about taking the trash out or cleaning my room that had been ever-present when I last lived at home.

And, of course, because I didn't get home anywhere near often enough, I had to be sure to make the time to fit my friends into the mix. But I spent most of the time with my parents. My dad and I were at Big 5 Sporting Goods when the call came in. I recognized the number on my cellphone display. It was the generic switchboard number that shows up whenever anyone from the Idol office calls out. I'm not sure what I thought when I saw those all too familiar digits. I guess surprise, because I'd had no contact with anyone for the entire time I was home. It was the show's production manager asking me when I would be returning back to Los Angeles because they wanted me to go out on the audition tour. It was a no-brainer. I said yes there and then, and told him I'd be back in Los Angeles in a few days and I'd swing by the office the day after I returned so we could sort stuff out. I hung up knowing that the hell I'd put myself through had paid off. I still had a job. That made it easy to enjoy the rest of my trip home, and enjoy my dad's bragging about his son who worked in TV.

GOING TO THE BALL

I was invited to my first Hollywood wedding soon after the finale.

We've already established the fact that I am a jeans and T-shirt guy, meaning I had nothing to wear. I mean seriously I didn't even own a pair of slacks let alone dress pants. You can't go to a wedding in jeans and a T-shirt, it just isn't the *done* thing. There were street people better dressed than me back then. I was being paid in pennies on the show. There was no residual income or discretionary spend or whatever the posh words for spare money are these days. I simply didn't have the cash to splash on a suit, or even a decent pair of shoes for that matter. And of course, no one working on the show was close to my size so I couldn't exactly ask to borrow anything that wouldn't leave me looking like Little Orphan Annie in my hand-me-downs. And let's be honest, I didn't fancy admitting I wasn't grown up enough to own a suit. We'll not even mention the fact that I was ashamed I couldn't afford a cheap one.

And then, after a few days of stewing and wondering how the hell I was going to politely blow off the wedding without hurting people's feelings, I remembered Ryan. Not, of course that I was going phone up the host and say, "Hey dude, can you do me a solid? Lend a guy a pair of slacks, would ya?" It wasn't as though I needed to ask, after all. His entire wardrobe, every item of clothing he'd worn throughout the season hung in the wardrobe room on the third floor.

So what the hell, I figured I would take a look. We were about the same height, but he's a lot chunkier than I am. There's a lot of talk of weight obsession in our society, and it's almost always directed at the size zero models and the unreasonable image of womanhood they feed into the machinery of the press, screwing with the heads of perfectly beautiful women - imagine Botticelli without his ample breasts and folds of cherubic flesh to paint! But what folks don't seem to realize is that the obsession hits both sexes just as unreasonably.

Ryan was obsessed with food and how his body looked. For a while he was afraid of eating carbohydrates and clung to a diet of fish, well, mainly sushi from the sushi restaurant he invested in down the road from the studio, and grilled chicken salads. Every now and again he'd jones for a donut or muffin and when he succumbed he'd allow himself the luxury of a bite, chew to drain the thing of all flavor, then spit it out.

I guess that answers the eternal question of does he spit or swallow.

Our host doesn't swallow.

So there's a healthy eating disorder right there.

Not that I particularly cared one way or the other. The guy was a cocky little shit, too good to say hello to anyone. Of course, you might spot the snide jab at the guy's sexuality there, maybe I'm just uncomfortable when guys are prettier than the females around them, or maybe it was because he spent so much time obsessing about how he looked and dressed, or maybe it was the constant chatter that he was supposedly banging his hairdresser, Dean. I didn't buy the Dean thing. I still don't. Sure, they were close, Dean took it upon himself to act as Ryan's personal security guard most of the time, but I couldn't figure the dynamics of it. I mean, Ryan's a tiny guy and Dean's a beast of man who you'd expect to find in the castle at the top of the beanstalk... it just didn't *fit*. I know it sounds dumb, but I just couldn't visualize it. Add to that, Ryan wasn't exactly swimming in female flesh, and the women that did hang around had that Vegas call girl chic going on and it's no surprise people liked to talk. Hell, they've got to talk about something, right?

So come that fateful day, I arrived a good half an hour before I typically did. I found the key to the room, snuck up there and started rifling the racks. I felt like Daddy Bear, everything was too small or too big and I was looking for just right. I'd smuggled up a black garbage sack just in case I found Goldilocks' suit and needed to smuggle it to my car. I didn't want to be caught 'borrowing'. Here's the thing, I know zero about clothes. I couldn't tell you a designer from off-the-rack and couture sounds like something that grows on old cheese. So I flipped through the racks blindly looking for something that appealed to me. In the end I found a gray suit with white pin stripes. It was a little too big, but I tried it on hopefully. It fit pretty well and looked half-decent so in the bag it went, and Cinders got to go to the ball.

And after the ball I forgot all about Ryan's borrowed suit and left it hanging in my closet.

THE UGLY, THE FAT AND THE FIRED

First day back in L.A. I turned up bright and early.
Everyone was in prep mode.
There would be two production coordinators going out on the road, me and the guy who was the head production assistant from Season 3. He was responsible for hiring production assistants in the various cities we hit along the way. My remit was a little less focused, which is a polite way to say my responsibilities were all over the board. I was dealing with employee paperwork, logistics, including the shipping of all the office supplies as well as on set essentials like walkie-talkies, tape stock, and basically anything that required assistance from Fedex. I was also in charge of catering and was venue liaison, making sure everything that needed to be in place was in place.

A few weeks earlier he'd been above me on the totem pole, now I was shouldering twice, three times as much work and very much obviously a step above him. The production manager admitted that the guy had only been hired because he was tall as strong as the proverbial ox, but the guy was as dumb as a bag of nails. Actually, he admitted he suspected the man had some sort of disability, and he'd made a mistake (and paid for it through the usual battery of verbal abuse from our beloved leader) hiring him instead of me. Apparently he'd wanted to hire me from the Season 2 auditions, and then again from Season 2's Hollywood Week, but he'd listened to the producers and paid for it through the entire Season 3.

It was nice to hear something positive after all the verbals from Wylleen the Hutt. A few well-chosen words inspired me more than all the smack-downs put together. My response? Hell, I really wanted to show the ox up, then maybe, just maybe, I'd get the offer to jump into his grave, I mean job, once the audition tour was over.

I was going to shine.

But I had all these new duties and no one told me what I was supposed to be doing. Sure they'd told me what was expected of me but I wasn't given a handbook or a crib sheet about how to get things done or who to call, or well, anything really. I was just expected to know. I was the boy with the deer heart staring down the headlights with my giant eyes and that damned stupid look on my face.

My full on-the-job training consisted of being told to get a couple binders, a legal pad and pen, and jump.

What else could I do? I closed my eyes and jumped down the rabbit hole. And thank fuck nothing remotely exciting happened, at least not while we were still all in the office putting the audition tour together. Nothing exciting is good. It's what I lived for. I spent most of my days on the phone.

The whole hiring practice was... an experience. I wasn't part of it, but I saw it going on all around me. Let's just say it scared me every now and then. The production assistants that were hired for the road were found on Craigslist. Fairly generic ads were placed on the site. They said something like an L.A. based production was coming to town and needed to hire a certain amount of production assistants for the duration of the show's stay. The show was never named because we wanted people who actually wanted to work to apply, rather than people who were gossip whores and wannabe celebutards with no real desire to work, but instead wanted to just be a part of the circus.

It wasn't my job, so I wasn't about to stick my nose in, but it wasn't as if the odd alarm bell didn't ring. No one knew these people. No one knew what they were like. No one knew if they were serial killers, molesters, psychos, thieves, nutbars or anything of the many colorful shades of batshit crazy in between.

And, of course, references were never checked.

The typical hiring process was a single phone call in which my fellow production coordinator would get a resume, call the number that the person sent along and ask them the sixty-four thousand dollar question: are you available to work. If the answer was yes, they were hired. No more questions asked.

It was standard operating procedure to hold a production meeting on the day we arrived in a new city (or the day after if we couldn't get it sorted that day). The production meeting would last a couple hours and each new production assistant hire would be placed in a position for the week. Criterion for the various duties was based on age, size, and race. The more mobile guys were given the positions where being fleet of foot was advantageous. The heavier boys and less athletic ones were given desk jobs where they could sit all day long. And, because there were always some that just didn't fit what we were looking for, they were given the jobs that would only last a day or two, if that.

What goes around comes around, right? Karma's a bitch, and all that jazz. We'll we were treated like shit in the office, so we treated the temporary hires in the mobile office like shit. Every day the auditions got smaller and smaller because there were fewer contestants around to audition. We'd switch between venues going from larger halls to more intimate ones, using the move as an excuse to weed out the ugly, the fat, and the just plain dumb production assistants. So even though they were told they would be used for the entire week there just wasn't the work for them. When they'd filed their paperwork for the day they were told, "Thanks, we're done with you. No need to come back."

There's something really off about judging people by age, size, or race, but that was the recommended breakdown for every production assistant hire on the audition road. Age, size, race. Y'know there ought to be a law against that sort of discrimination. Oh, wait, there is, isn't there?

And, no illusions being shattered here: just as the ugly, the fat, and the dumb were let go right away, the pretty, the skinny, and most definitely the slutty, were asked to stay the entire week, and stuff like work ethic be damned. Who cared if they actually pulled their weight, they looked good, right? Just so long as the executives were happy with their slutty eye-candy we were golden.

There were always exceptions that prove the rule, of course. So the few standouts from the original group hire, be they male or female, pretty or pig ugly, fat or disgustingly thin, were kept around for the entire week. Someone had to get the work done, after all.

THE BEST SLEEP I EVER GOT

And, of course, we perpetuated the lies told to us when we'd started.

During the city stops for both the Season 4 and Season 5 auditions we spouted the same lies to the production assistants that we'd been told. We said they would be working no more than a twelve hour days, hell more like ten, don't sweat it. It didn't matter that there was no possible way to gauge how long each day would last without a crystal ball – I mean we didn't know how many people would turn up to audition until we were neck deep in auditions.

The day's structure was based around the auditions. The more hopefuls that showed up, the longer the day. It was a pretty simple equation.

Sure, back in L.A. the notion of twelve hour workdays was fairly common, but out on the road it wasn't. So the lies were necessary to stop the workers from revolting. Not that it helped much when you told them, don't sweat it, we're talking ten hours really, and wanted them to clock fifteen in an entirely different version of reality. Most folks that were hired couldn't imagine working ten hour shifts, so having told them what they needed to hear to sign up we got used to the giant shit fits that followed when the lifting and carrying started.

Two hours max would often turn into four or five more hours and it wasn't uncommon for production assistants to walk out on the job or just not show up the next morning for work.

You developed a sixth sense (not as in I see dead people...or maybe it was a bit like that come to think of it) for who would or wouldn't show up the next morning. The biggest 'tell' was when they'd ask you to review their paperwork packet and make sure that everything was signed off and filled out completely. Hell, I didn't blame them. I'd thought about just not turning up plenty of times, and I walked off the job in Greensboro during Season 5 as I was just too fucking exhausted to work an eighth day in the week, having done a bare minimum of sixteen hour days for the last couple of months. Not only was the flesh not able, the spirit seriously wasn't willing. I understood what it meant to be exhausted, properly exhausted. I'd been tired plenty of times in my life, but now, now I was done. I was falling apart physically and mentally. I'd blacked out at my desk in the production office with my chin resting on my computer, eyes closed and arms out in front of me. A security guard flicked one of my ears with his middle finger. That was my rude awakening in more ways than one. I packed up my computer, grabbed my backpack and the keys to one of the passenger vans, and walked out without saying a word to anyone about where I was going. I killed my cellphone and headed back to the hotel where I proceeded to fall asleep for the next several hours. It was quite possibly the best sleep I had ever gotten. After waking up I eventually headed back to the venue and continued with the day.

No, I couldn't blame them at all.

BROWN BAGGING IT

And of course there were more lies used to keep the wheels greasy.

On their last day, the hired-in production assistants were told they'd receive their check within a week, by which time, of course the show would have moved on to pastures new. So when they didn't get their checks we weren't on hand for all the complaints. And of course the checks were never on hand because it took up to two weeks for all the paperwork to be processed and signed off on, and then sent to Los Angeles to be processed, then the checks would be cut and mailed out. So in general folks were looking at a month before they saw their cash.

I knew what it was like to be on the receiving end of that kind of wheel-greasing lie a time or two myself, so I couldn't help but feel a little sympathy for these guys. I remembered all too well what it was like, to be honest. Production assistants were always the last to eat on the road, left to scrape up the scraps because there was never much left by the time they were allowed to eat.

There was a reason for that, and it goes right back to Occam and his most obvious answers: saving as much money as possible. I was told to under order every meal. If there were seventy employees, I ordered for fifty. If there were one hundred ordered for seventy-five. There was never enough food for everyone to get a decent meal. After a couple of days on-set the smarter production assistants started to bring their own snacks. Some of them even brown-bagged it. That way, at least, they got to eat.

THE KEEPER OF THE SECRETS

We started in Cleveland and on the first night in the city ended up at the Stripper Graveyard down on the waterfront somewhere. It was like an elephant graveyard, but instead of elephants, it's this seedy place where strippers went to die.

As appealing as the notion of zombie strippers is, when it comes right down to the bump and grind, it takes a special sort of desperate to want a disease-riddled drug addicted crotch inches from your face. There were only so many overpriced drinks I could take, and alas, they weren't burning out my eyes, so I got up and walked out.

Outside, as the cold air hit me, I realized that I had no idea where the hell I was, and more to the point, how the hell I was going to get back to the hotel.

I stood around in the dark for a while, watching the headlights roll by until a cab finally took mercy on me. Once back in the hotel bed I passed out, shoes and everything else still on. Although the show had two production managers, only one went out on the road during the auditions. Adderall Porn Guy came out on the road with us, while his counterpart stayed back in the office setting up stuff for the next city, hiring local camera and audio crews, pulling permits and dealing with the contracts for the venues.

In all honesty he and I, along with the other production

coordinator, were the only three people from the production side of the show. There was the contestant coordinator who by this time had become my partner in crime. She was brilliant and our bond was stronger than ever. Another thing we had in common was that we weren't really 'people persons' erm 'people people' I guess that should be. Anyway, we really didn't enjoy the company of many of the guys on the staff, so whenever the opportunity arose – and we had the time – we'd play hooky and sneak away to do our own thing.

More often than not, we'd grab dinner or a drink, and generally we'd make a point of not bothering to invite anyone else.

We weren't unfriendly, we were nice enough, I think, in that we didn't go out of our away to avoid anyone, said hi, you know, but deep down neither of us really cared for many of them. You know the deal. We all work with people we don't like but don't dislike. And, as sleazy as it sounds, we were nice to the ones we needed to be nice to. As contestant coordinator she was responsible for all things 'contestant'. She had to meet with each of them from day one and make sure they signed the proper release forms before allowing them to get their sticker ID number for auditioning. If they made it to the next round they would have to go see her again, and fill out more paperwork, and then some more paperwork for subsequent auditions, the sort of stuff pertaining to when and where they would come back to audition for the executive producers. If they made it through that round they'd meet with her again, and she'd give them the next hoop to jump through, meaning when they had to come back and audition for the actual judges.

She had a lot of pressure on her shoulders day-in and day-out. She was the keeper of the secrets. She knew everything about everyone, every last little bit of their personal information. Take a second to imagine the repercussions if she ever happened to lose any of it? We're talking celebrity stalker paradise. Hey, maybe that could be a new song for Coolio?

PARTING THE RED SEA

The first actual day of auditions – and maybe this was foreshadowing what was going to come – in Cleveland I was awoken at four a.m. by my cellphone. I rolled out and grabbed it off the nightstand. It was the production manager.

My first thought was that something was wrong. Phones don't ring at four in the morning unless there's something wrong. I was sleep-fuzzy. We'd made a deal: he'd arrive at the venue around four and I'd sleep 'til six, then we'd rotate on and off with this schedule during the auditions. He was in a complete panic, hyperventilating on the other end of the line. It took me a moment to make sense of his blather through the ragged breathes, but so many contestants had arrived that the venue was already panicking about capacity and safety concerns. They'd have to open the place early to let the contestants in. It was a mess. There was no other way to keep everyone safe. The sheer volume of people that had turned up had completely taken everyone by surprise so it was all hands to the pumps. I rolled out of bed, showered in record speed, and headed down to the venue. I gathered up a bunch of other employees. No one was being allowed to sleep in. We crowded into the fifteen passenger van. I was the designated driver.

I couldn't make it into the underground parking area, the

contestants were everywhere. Hell, I couldn't even make it halfway around the building without having to lean on the horn. I felt like Moses trying to part the Red Sea. It took us thirty minutes to get around the side of the building and into the parking garage.

And we hadn't even started day one.

I'm not a big believer in signs, portents, prognostications or any other form of fortune telling, but right then I just knew we were seeing the shape of things to come.

THE SECURITY BLANKET

What I hadn't counted on was the escalation of my Number 2's Adderall addiction.

I don't think he actually slept. Hell, he probably had a big crayon-portrait in his attic back home that was stoned out of its mind every day while he aged disgracefully. The guy was one permanent ball of drug-fueled energy. He couldn't sit still for more than twenty seconds before he started twitching and needed to be up again and moving.

Midway through the audition tour, he took me aside for a five minute confessional, as though he expected me to absolve him of his sins. His confession? Back at the Stripper's Graveyard he'd paid good money for one of the undead to do more than bump and grind on his lap. I assume the drugs were the only reason he managed to get it up, because having seen the crotch-rot that pretended to be pussy I couldn't imagine any cock being willing. Talk about going above and beyond the cause. His dick deserved a Purple Heart. I begged him to spare me the gory details. I really didn't want the image of him banging away, all hyped up on Adderall while zombie stripper-hooker moaned and writhed and did the Monster Mash beneath him.

Barely a few short days into the audition tour it was obvious that the stress of the job was already getting to the production manager. He started begging off any social contact, and instead locked himself away in his hotel room, ordered room service, and jerked off to help relieve his stress. And trust me, I wish I didn't know about his proclivities, but that particular smell is pretty damned unique, and just one time I made the mistake of opening his door, but one time was all it took. I'm pretty sure the cleaner was risking pregnancy just by walking into the room, there was so much semen in the air. There were other smells too, very old Caesar Salad dressing, dirty clothes laced with body odor so thick it had begun to crust and a few pairs of old dirty gym socks thrown into the mix. But the post-jerk-off sweat overpowered the rest of the mix.

And the poor bastard looked worse that the room smelled.

He sat at the dressing table wearing old dirty workout shorts and a T-shirt that might have been white once but now looked like a pearl-crusted cum rag. I had this crazy image of Linus and his security blanket and couldn't shake it. Our boy didn't have a security blanket, he had a security cum rag. Even now the whole thing just gives me the heebie jeebies. How much cum could a cum rag hold if a cum rag could hold cum? All the evidence suggested a damn sight more than the loving spoonful or 10cc's. But then, he'd had a lifetime to soak it up. The guy was unshaven and glassy eyed, with a serious case of bed head going on. To say I was hesitant about entering the room is a bit like saying the Pope's a bit religious. I might not have been able to get knocked-up off the stench, but I was pretty sure a dozen communicable diseases were floating around in the stale air and I really didn't fancy becoming Patient Zero for the zombie plague.

The place was a mess. Stiff hotel towels piled up beside his bed. Room service trays and dirty plates were stacked in every free space around the room.

It was the same in every hotel room across the country that summer.

The Do Not Disturb sign hung on every door, while behind them the dirty dishes, the crusty sheets and the filthy clothes piled up.

After a couple of weeks of this, I broached the idea of having the L.A. based production manager fly out to take up some of the load. We're all the same deep down, we hate the notion of losing face or admitting weakness. So, of course, he gave this full-on bluster about how it wasn't that hard for him, that he had it covered, when really he just didn't want to look like a pussy – even a zombified one 'fresh' from the Stripper's Graveyard – because that'd be the first nail in his coffin, and while sometimes they came back, washed out production managers didn't.

RUBBER WRISTBAND BOMB

It wasn't uncommon for the production manager and a couple guys from the security team to travel ahead to the next city and start prepping things for our arrival. It was like going to war, sending in advance recon to scout out the lie of the land, meet people that needed to be met, that sort of stuff.

That's what happened with Washington DC that year.

After the final round of judging in Cleveland, me and the fellow production coordinator were left to break everything down and pack it away to be shipped on to DC. It was a relatively simple process, and by now we'd done it more times than we could count on our hands so it was just a case of going through the motions while the others headed on to the airport.

Remember I said I wasn't big on prognostication? Well, maybe there's a time and a place for believing in signs. Folks touched down in DC and pretty much immediately realized that they were in way over their heads. If Cleveland had been busy, the sheer amount of hopefuls turning up for the auditions in DC was akin to a military invasion. We'd gotten pretty accustomed to thinking on our feet, and rather adept at last minute changes, but Washington DC put all of our collective ingenuity to the test.

The frazzled production manager called me and told me to

just grab as many wristbands as I could and get my ass on the next plane.

We were well used to the hopefuls lining up early desperate to get to the front of the audition queue, so we'd walk the line and dish out wristbands well ahead of time to keep the crowds from hanging around the venues and just getting in the way. The wristbands never held a place in line – they weren't magic – but they did secure your spot to audition, and for most people that was enough.

I grabbed a few thousand wristbands and rushed back to the hotel to pack, check out, and hightail it to the airport. As usual, I was clueless when it came to the actual details. We were never big on the details. Practicalities? Pah! I had no idea if I there was a ticket booked under my name or if I was expected to be on standby.

Leaping into a cab I called the travel coordinator back in Los Angeles. She'd booked me the last ticket on next flight and I was to rush, to hell with red lights, if I had to I was to murder my way through to the front of the check-in line and demand that I be allowed on the flight regardless of the fact that there was no way I could possibly arrive at the airport in adequate time for takeoff.

The thing is, that guy, the kind of ass who runs red lights, pushes to the front of the line and makes a scene... that just isn't me. The suggestion was laughable, really. I couldn't demand a beer from a bartender, I had to smile and chat and almost apologize for putting them out.

I tried to object, but the travel coordinator steamrollered over me. I was to use the name of *American Idol* in vain. I was supposed to excuse all of my bad behavior with the classic "I'm with Idol, it's a showbiz emergency. I have to be on that next flight."

It wasn't the first time I'd been fed crap like that, but it always shocked me. There was this wonderful Hollywood logic that everything Idol was that important the rest of the world was supposed to stand aside, or drop everything, to keep us happy. It was a matter of national importance. It was Idol, damnit! To hell with how it affected them, their job, or anyone around them. It was Idol!

But I did what I was told. I pushed, I shoved, I jumped the line and invoked the unholy name of Idol at the desk and made it onto the flight, the last seat on the plane, which wasn't even a proper seat, it was the jump seat (a single seat in the front row.) I was the last person on the plane, and got my fair share of the evil eye as I took my seat.

But for all that, there was one priceless moment at security that made all the bullshit and all the rushing worthwhile. Customs guys threw my backpack into the scanner and didn't have a clue what they were looking at on their x-ray machine so they pulled me aside. I must have looked like a shoe-bomber, sweating, out-of-breath, having run way past the point of my endurance to get to the gate, clutching the backpack like it was the most precious thing in the world. And hell, I was a last, last, last minute entry onto the flight. Prime terrorist suspect stuff, I'm sure. So, the security guy pops the clasps on my backpack not sure what the hell to expect as he opened it. What he sure as shit didn't expect was for thousands of rubber wristbands to explode in his face. There were so many of the damned things packed in tight they just flew out all over the place when the clasps were released. The poor guy ducked, I'm sure expecting the explosion to follow the rubber bands and tear his face off, and I burst out laughing. We're talking manic laughter, like his panic was the funniest thing I had ever seen.

When he recovered, he asked me why I was transporting thousands of rubber wristbands and I, of course, had to tell him they were for *American Idol.*

Some terrorist I'd make. Interrogation? I'd crack under the first question.

BANK FEES AND MY TWO NEW ASSHOLES

Even before I reached the hotel's reception desk I had a dour-faced brute of security guard in my face, hand out, asking me for the wristbands. I couldn't have felt more like a drug mule if I'd tried. Still, right then all I wanted to do was sleep, so I handed the goods over.

One of the 'perks' of not being addicted to prescription drugs was that I actually slept. Another was that I was given the responsibility of dealing with the petty cash for the show while we were on the audition tour. Petty cash ain't so petty when you're talking about something as big as Idol. Believe me. At any given time I had thousands of dollars on me, stuffed into the bottom of my backpack ripe for a mugging or just light fingers.

Anyone with half a brain still functioning would have hated having to account for the petty cash, hell if I didn't have enough for the Executive Producer's Starbucks every morning it was a tarring and feathering offense. It was my fault. It didn't matter what the truth of the situation was, the blame had to land somewhere and I had a big petty cash-shaped target painted on my back. Standard operating procedure involved me being given a check for around ten thousand dollars once a week and having to find a local bank to cash it. Not so hard, banks are a dime a dozen, right? Well, yeah, but I think we've already established the show was cheap when it came to the stupidest little costs that could be cut and would rather I'd drive around blowing thirty bucks of gas (and an hour plus of the cost of my wages) than cash the check at a bank that would charge me a fee for the privilege of doing so.

I banked at Wells Fargo, so come every new city, I tried my damnedest to find a Wells Fargo, but sometimes I just wasn't able to. Like now. So I bit the bullet and let the bank charge me a few dollars to cash the petty cash check. We're talking less than ten bucks here from a 10k check.

These ten bucks earned me a world of hurt when I was ripped not one, but two brand news assholes over them.

MONEY FAIRIES

Washington DC was by far and away the toughest city on the audition tour.

The crowds were huge, and every step of the way they'd been underestimated, meaning we didn't have enough security, we didn't have enough assistants, and all the rest of it. Everyone panicked. And I mean everyone. The venue itself was vast. I mean it took dozens of city blocks to fully cross from end to end, and the production office was all the way in the far back of the building, up a flight of stairs so we could see the hopefuls as they filed in and lined up the night before the auditions.

I said it was a nightmare, right? Two things off the top of my head that I remember: there were so many contestants there already the night before the audition we actually ran out of portable toilets. We also ran out of barricades meaning we couldn't keep everyone in line and stop idiots from cruising to the front.

I was told to empty the petty cash envelope and hand it over to the production manager so he could order more portable toilets and miles of barricading and be able to pay cash for it. It had to be cash. The need was desperate and we could not afford to wait a day or two for the transactions to take place before a check was cut to the company and mailed out from Los Angeles (which is what happened when everything was ordered and paid for in advance). So this cleaned out my petty cash. I had a fistful of dollars left until the next check arrived, which was currently being overnighted from Los Angeles to the hotel. In the meantime we needed cash for all those sundry little expenses that popped up throughout the day, and being in charge of the petty cash everyone just expected me to head over to the nearest ATM and withdraw several hundred dollars of my own money to cover it until the check arrived. Hell no, was the polite answer to that one. And of course my refusal to help the show out made it all the way back to Wylleen the Hutt.

As soon as my phone rang I knew exactly who it was and what was going to happen next. She was never able to resist the opportunity to exercise her potty mouth. I answered the phone. I barely managed to say "Hello" before I was spit-roasted like a hula pig in Hawaii.

"You need to get your ass to the bank and take care of this money problem, Bucks. You're in charge of petty cash, that means you need to have cash on you at all times!"

I flat out refused. I mean point blank. I said no to a woman whose ears, by some fluke of evolutionary design, were genetically disposed to filtering out everything apart from the affirmative. Still, valiantly, I told her that hell would freeze over before I covered show expenses from my own bank account. I tried logic, pointing out that if anyone should be doing it, surely it was the production manager as he was in a higher position me. Logic didn't work. She can be very creative when it comes to finding ways to insult someone. And when her creative well finally ran dry she resorted to the good old standby "piece of shit" she was so fond of. The only thing that stopped me from hanging up was that I wanted to keep my job. Finally, she hung up. I didn't cave in. They weren't getting a cent from me.

I don't know where the money came for the rest of the day, but as if by magic the production manager ended up with several hundred dollars in his hand.

Maybe it was the fairies?

A WALL OF SILENCE

When the petty cash check arrived at the hotel the following morning, I grabbed it and headed over to the venue to check on my duties before leaving to search for a bank that would cash the check without charging me a fee.

It was never going to be that easy though.

I hadn't been on-site more than five minutes when I was told that we'd had some 'incidents' among the contestants who'd slept there overnight because they wanted to be the first to audition in the morning.

Incidents...

That's a fucking spineless way of putting it. One of the so-called incidents was that one girl had fled in the middle of the night after being gang-raped in one of the restrooms by a group of guys. The other was a fight that had broken out between a group of girls. One of them smashed a glass bottle and slashed out with it threatening to cut the other girls if they continued on with whatever they were doing.

It was the production manager's job to liaise with the police and deal with this stuff, but he didn't. No one did. Hell, the entire crew developed an ostrich mentality, burying their heads in the sand and seemingly thinking, "If no one mentions it maybe it'll just go away"

Over the course of the night several people had also been

removed by security for stealing purses and money from other contestants.

But I couldn't get the girl who said she had been gang raped in the restroom out of my mind.

I asked around, but it was like coming up against walls of 'couldn't care less'. "Yeah, I heard something about that," was the most I'd get out of people. Everyone seemed to have heard something but no one seemed to know anything.

And no one seemed all that bothered about finding out the truth.

The nonchalance made me sick to the stomach.

A FEE AND A VICTORY

I had to leave. I needed fresh air. Air not tainted by the show or anything remotely connected to the show.

I grabbed the petty cash check, shouldered my backpack and headed out on my own to try to find that bank.

I asked the lady who was our contact for the venue where she though would be best to deal with this. I guess my mind was elsewhere because I stepped outside and took the wrong direction at the first possible opportunity. I hadn't been gone for more than five minutes before my phone rang. I checked the display knowing it would be the generic studio number. It was. It was Jabba herself calling to cut me open and smear lemon juice into the wound. This time she couldn't believe that I'd abandoned everyone. Why wasn't I at the venue helping to deal with the rape and the fight? Why had I left the production manager there alone?

"Where the hell are you?" I was asked.

"I am going to cash the petty cash check and then head back to the venue."

"I cannot believe you left him there to deal with all the bullshit that's going on. What kind of fucking employee are you?" And already, three sentences in to the 'conversation' she was screaming.

I adopted my usual sarcastic tone reserved especially for

dealing with morons. "A good one."

I could feel the heat down the phone line from her getting redder and reader. I could picture her swelling up with anger like some giant blowfish.

"And Mister Good Employee What the fuck are you doing that so god damn important that you're not helping to deal with the situation?"

"I am out walking around Washington DC going from bank to bank to see if any of them will cash my petty cash check without charging me a minimal fee to do so." I couldn't help myself, despite everything I enjoyed throwing that out there.

I could hear her sigh and take a deep breath. I was pushing her buttons.

"You do know we're out of money right?" I asked, not giving her the chance to vent more spleen.

"Yes."

"So I need to find bank to cash the check. I can help out when I get back. But, just so you know, no one seemed all that cut up so that's why I left to deal with this." I said.

"Just go to the nearest bank and cash the check and get back to the venue!"

I waited a beat. "What about the fee?"

"Fee? For fuck's sake just cash the fucking check! I never said you had to find a bank that wouldn't charge, just that I would prefer you to."

"Oh, great. Thanks so much. You just made it a lot easier." I said.

"Just get back to the fucking venue." She hung up.

I reveled in my pettiness. It felt fantastic to throw that crap about fees in her face, even though it was only a small victory, and wouldn't last very long, I was determined to savor it. I found a bank, cashed the check, made damned sure they charged me before I headed back to the venue with a little skip in my step.

ONE VOICE

During the final judging round with Simon, Paula, and Randy one of the employee's mothers came into town to help out for the last few days. It was love at first sight. She was just this fantastically tightly wound package of mom fun who was most certainly not afraid to be the life and soul of the party when called upon.

She hung out with us for a couple days and we bonded. We're not talking hanky-panky but there was a good connection, better by far than I shared with 95% of the crew. Come to think of it, I'd also gotten on fairly well with her daughter, so I guess being nice ran in the genes.

Even so, I had no idea what was coming once we reached the airport.

We were heading on to the next city, mom was heading home.

While we were waiting she pulled me aside and things turned serious.

She looked me in the eye and asked me to promise her I'd keep an eye on her little girl because she was, and I quote, being sexually harassed on a daily by one of the producers. We talked in serious, urgent, hushed tones. She confided in me. She told me that it was making her daughter physically ill. She was so uncomfortable she'd call her mom every night and just cry her eyes out as she told her the stuff she'd gone through that day.

And it was every night. Things had gotten worse and worse the longer we were on the road.

I'll tell you what, this woman showed incredible restraint. In her place I'd have just gone over to the guy and ripped his balls off sans anesthetic. But as with any case of bullying, and make no mistake, that's what it was, the victim is always the one left worrying that things will only escalate should anyone find out and try to help. The bully – the abuser – would just lash out and try to make her life even more of a misery, and her mom really didn't want that.

Hell, the woman was taking a chance by telling *me* this stuff, I mean I could easily have been in the producer's pocket, a company man, but her girl needed a friend on the inside. Someone who could play interference if the bastard had her cornered. Mom said she didn't know how far the harassment had gone, but she had her suspicions. The only things she confirmed were that her daughter had to put up with hearing how great her breasts looked and how he could teach her something if she'd let him in her pants. You know, the usual sleazoid stuff that counts as bad dialogue in a porn movie.

Here's the thing: I knew the producer, or at least I knew him by rumor. He had a reputation for sending text messages and photos of himself. You can fill in the blanks, but let's just say nothing would have surprised me by now. One of the last things her mom said to me was that I had her permission to beat the living shit out of the guy if ever wanted to, and that she'd cover any medical bills and legal fees the beating incurred. She said it with a smile, like she was joking, but like all good humor it had its basis in the truth. She wanted me to beat his worthless ass, and you know what? I'm not going spout some sanctimonious shit about being a lover not a fighter, or doing the macho bang my chest bullshit, here's the truth: I would have done it in a heartbeat if he'd given me the slightest provocation. If I'd walked in on them in a compromising position. Anything. And believe me, I looked out for her for the rest of her time on the show. But I didn't see anything. Bullies and abusers are smart like that. They have a sixth sense for when it's safe to do their bullying.

A couple of years later I asked the daughter about the guy, and what had happened, and she told me everything, backing up what her mom had said, and she explained why she never did anything. It was the same reason so many women don't do anything when this shit kicks off around them, and it makes me hate my own sex, because of course she never said anything because she didn't think anyone would believe her, and the potential repercussions were too great. She'd get a reputation and would never have been able to find work in Los Angeles. What production company would want to hire her? I tell you, Hollywood's one of the last real bastions of what they call the Man's World, and sometimes men just plain suck.

I'll be candid. I was really disappointed she didn't stand up for herself. I mean I can understand what she had to lose, but every girl out there stands to lose the same thing, and someone has to hold dirtbags like this guy responsible for his actions. She was violated. The world only becomes a better place when people stand up for themselves. One voice, that's all it takes. One voice, and others will take up the cry. They will. I honestly believe that. I need to believe that, because the alternative would destroy any lingering faith I have in humanity.

THE HOBBLING

Random acts of senseless violence, that's what I'll remember when I think of Washington, DC. If something could go wrong, it did go wrong. If an argument could break out, it broke out. The crew got into fights. Drugs were imbibed, and many, many miles were walked.

As stupid as it sounds when put side by side with alleged gang rape in the toilet and sexual harassment, the one thing I remember more vividly than anything else that happened in DC are the blisters. My feet literally bled through the dozen blisters and weeping sores that ruined them. The damned things took forever to heal. I felt like Paul Sheldon, the hero of Stephen King's Misery, about thirty minutes after Annie Wilkes had taken the hammer to his ankles and hobbled him. I still feel phantom-limb pain from those damned blisters...

THE CHANNEL-SURFING THREESOME

While we were in Washington DC the L.A. based production manager flew out to make a surprise appearance.

None of us grunts knew she was coming, but it didn't take us long to figure out that our traveling production manager was too ashamed to admit that the circus was too much for him to handle alone. In typical Idol-fashion she was given less than twenty-four hours notice that she would be leaving Los Angeles and living out of a suitcase for the foreseeable future.

It was good to have her around and she seemed as though she actually wanted to be there.

Mind you, she did enjoy some of the perks that came with being on the road, namely the 'what happens in (insert random city name) stays in (insert same random city name)' mentality. Her sexual appetite was insatiable, and she had a thing for the muscular, chiseled members of the security team. It wasn't uncommon for her to have the odd sleepover in her hotel room. She had a gift, she could sweet-talk every hotel into giving her an upgrade, sometimes wrangling as much as a suite out of them, because as she rationalized it, it was the least they could do for us. Our rolling Idol Tour Party was bringing in a small fortune for the various hotels we hit along the way.

The only time I visited her room, I found her sprawled out

on the bed with two security guards (brothers by the way, so you go girl, nail the set,) one on either side of her idly flipping through the channels. I'm not so sexually naïve that I don't know a threesome when I see one. There's a way people have of interacting, touching, connecting, once they've been intimate, it's easy, familiar. It's instantly recognizable. They had that manner.

THE SECURITY CASTING COUCH

And apropos of security guards caught inflagrante delicto...

The show's whole security set-up was shambolic.

We're talking giant man-boys, butched-up guys in their mid-twenties with one mission in life: the quest for the perfect pussy.

There were tricks to it, of course. Some of the guys were initiates of The Game, Neil Strauss' book on how to hunt, snare and kill, or in this case, screw, helpless women in the big bad city. It's a serial man-slut's bible. The book is like a self-help guide to getting laid. Anyway, I was fascinated by how our security boys went about the whole seduction thing. What was it Tom Cruise said in Magnolia? Respect the cock and tame the cunt. They had a game plan. Early on in the day they'd befriend one of the girls, just some chat, some smiles, nothing too overt, then the following day they would show her a few pictures on their cellphone, a little more chit and a bit of chat every now and then throughout the day. And on the third day they'd do the phone trick, 'accidentally' opening a file on their phone that contained nude pictures of themselves or short videos of them masturbating. The trick then was to act all shocked and embarrassed and quickly close the photo application and apologize over and over again, so it looked as if they really didn't mean to do that. This was their oh-so-subtle way of testing the water. If the girls didn't object to the picture show they more often than not had them in bed before the end the day. If they did object then they just moved on to another one until they could find one that was comfortable playing. It was numbers game. Try it enough times and you'd get a hit. The trick was to be working on several different girls at the same time. If one, two or even three blew them out, four, five or six might just blow them...

And, of course, they took the show's name in vain, invoking the unholy promise of how they might just be able to get them a full-time job with the show once it was back in Los Angeles, and how they worked on several other shows so if it didn't work out with Idol, so there was always a chance it would with another show of theirs. You've seen the show, you can do the math, but we're talking four or five girls a week buying the line, seven cities on the audition tour, means thirty plus girls per guard who walked right on in to this lame-ass set-up, I would call them suckers, which of course they were, using multiple interpretations of the word, but worse than that, they were desperate, buying into the whole Hollywood Dream and giving a not-so entirely new lease of life to the casting couch... only now you didn't even have to be a director. All you needed was a nightstick and the cajones to get your pixilated cajones out.

HE COULD MAKE A HORSE JEALOUS

One of the more wryly amusing things about the show's security guards was how they would argue over who was going to watch over Simon. It was like watching a gaggle of giggly school girls fighting over who was going to be the first in line to see, buy, steal, whatever the latest obsession in the tween world was that week.

Seriously, it was hysterical to see these guys, and we're talking big, bulked-up and very masculine guys fighting about who was going to watch Simon. And it was a daily occurrence. Who isn't going to be curious, right? I mean, it's not normal, no matter how you try to rationalize it. He's not a real star, for fuck's sake, he's the star maker, so why all the fuss?

Finally, after a couple weeks of living with this whole thing, the not knowing was really bugging me, so I asked one of them what the big deal was with watching over Simon. "Oh, nothing, nothing, nothing," was the first response, and it had that absolute pitch-perfect coy school-girl-crush quality to it, you know, like the guy was flustered by the fact that I'd asked. Which just wasn't normal behavior. And it hadn't escaped my notice that none of them ever fought over Paula and Randy.

Sooooo, was I supposed to let it go when there were buttons

to be pushed? I wheedled, I begged, I groveled, threatened and blackmailed until he finally spilled the secret to me.

See, the security guard's main duty is to protect the show's talent. That translates to: they go everywhere with them. We're talking escorting them down from their rooms in the morning, making sure they got into their limos at the end of the day, and making sure the restrooms were clear before they went in.

With Simon, Randy, and Ryan the security guards followed them into the restrooms, with Paula they made sure the coast was clear before she went in, or one of her female entourage would go in with her.

So, why fight over Simon?

Okay, get this: they all loved looking at his dick. Yep, apparently they were fascinated by Simon Cowell's dick. Seems they loved to stand side-by-side with the guy in the urinal and glance over at it while he relieved himself. According to my guy, Mr. Cowell is hung like the proverbial horse. And now here I am propagating the myth that the guy is so big he has to fold it in half to get it into his underwear, but that's what my guy reckoned, and that was why they all fought for his security detail. The whole thing was just marginally bizarre. I mean here you had these butch security guards who spent their every waking minute chasing pussy, and yet they fought each other for the chance to steal a glimpse of Simon's cock in the restroom.

I guess that makes sense... in bizarro world.

PETTY CASH IS PRETTY CASH

I'd never visited New Orleans and had no idea what to expect. Well, that's not really true. I had lots of ideas of about what might be waiting down by Bourbon Street and around there. I'm as big a fan of drunken debauchery and sexual proclivity as the next man, and New Orleans is right up with Rio in terms of carnivals and parties. Hell, I loved the idea that you could drink in the streets without anyone batting an eyelash. Big Frank can keep New York, New Orleans is my kind of town.

Right after touch down the female production manager and I decided that we'd head into the city to grab some lunch while everyone else grabbed a few hours of sleep. Obviously, since it was our first time in town we headed straight for the Bourbon Street area and decided play eenie-meanie with the various restaurants, pick one and have lunch.

Even before I plonked my ass on the chair I knew what I wanted: one giant bowl of crawdads, which is what we called them in Oregon when I was growing up. Down here they were called crawfish. Like some sort of piscine psycho-killer I couldn't wait to tear the heads off and suck out the brain juice, then let the carnage begin (or being fish, should that be piscage, you know, given that carne means meat?)

My lunch date took a bit of convincing. It wasn't difficult

to tell she thought the entire idea was pretty gross, but I twisted her arm.

It was around this sort of time (with the prodding of the production managers) that I started to use the petty cash to indulge in the obligatory over-priced Starbucks for the three of us. We were fed up with the mulch that passed for coffee back in the hotels along the road and craved stuff that didn't taste like burnt molasses. Of course, everything is bright and shiny in the clarity of retrospect. The production managers were taking advantage of their position within the show, and had been for years, skimming a little here, a little there, and now they were bringing me into the fold. However you slice it, we were skimming (a polite way of saying stealing from the show) on a daily basis. We'd make up fake taxi receipts for one of the camera or audio guys to cover our tracks. It was a calculated risk, but given the relatively tiny amount of cash involved we knew the accountant wouldn't call them to confirm that they had indeed taken a taxi from point A to point B.

I felt like George Peppard telling Face Man and Howling Mad Murdoch that I loved it when a plan came together. The plan worked so well, in fact, that I started using petty cash to cover all my expenses on the road. We received a fifty dollar a day per diem to cover all food expenses and anything else that we wanted, but given how much they'd taken from me in unpaid wages the season before I decided that really wasn't enough.

And if one of the higher ups accused me? Well, then I'd throw the production managers under the bus. That's entertainment!

THE BITE MARKS OF MORONS

People are morons. And given the opportunity they'll always act like morons. It doesn't matter whether they wear designer suits and drive limited edition Lamborghinis or if they wear jeans and drive hybrids. You wonder why Hugh Grant crawled along that sidewalk to find Divine Brown when he had Liz Hurley at home? It's because people are morons. Why did R. Kelly make a sex tape or Pammy Anderson or any other B-List celebrity you care to mention who's gotten their hooch out on the Interweb? Because, my friends, people are morons.

When the circus rolls into a party town like New Orleans, it stands to reason that the combined brain cells of the crew take a vacation and priority number one from the moron brigade becomes getting as fucked up as possible, as quickly as possible. I told you, people are morons. I just wish I were joking.

After we finished our crawfish we were joined by most of the crew, including the two producers (who it turns out, in typical sleazy tabloid style, were sleeping together during the entire time on the road even though he was engaged and would be getting hitched when we returned to L.A.). She was a mess. But that was nothing new. The woman was particularly fond of the 'dirty white wife beater with black bra straps hanging out' ensemble. You can take the girl out of the trailer park, but you can't take the trailer park out of the girl. She had this ungainly walk that reminded me of horse, not a graceful stallion, not some powerful racehorse all bunched muscle and powerful limbs, more like one of the nags that takes kids for rides down on the beach. You know the sort, should have been sent to the glue factory years ago. In keeping with her horsiness, her tongue was too large for her mouth and used to loll out between her teeth while she sucked in air. She looked vaguely retarded. For the life of me, I can't see what anyone ever saw in her. The very idea of getting naked with her still sends shivers all the way down to the root of my soul. I would say she looked a little like Kelly Osbourne, but that's doing Ozzie's girl a disservice. Fairer to say she looked like a retarded version of Kelly after a three day long bender. And, classy lady that Trailer Park Producer was, she knew damn well that her on-the-road-Beau was engaged, of course she did, she was friends with the poor girl he was two-timing. But friendship isn't something that stops these people from fucking around. Like I said, people are morons.

Not that we needed to know shit about her inability to cum, but of course we heard all about it, repeatedly, and in glorious technicolor, and then when he finally rammed her all the way to paradise we were treated to a blow-by-blow that involved her leaving bite marks in the headboard in the New Orleans hotel. She was so proud of herself. Her first ever orgasm. Bite marks in the wooden headboard.

I listened to her sordid little tale, all the while trying to think of anything apart from her naked and on all fours. When she finished talking, breathless, horsey tongue hanging out, I said, "I am sure his fiancée would love to compare bite marks," and walked away.

CLIQUES

The female production manager celebrated her birthday while we were in town.

We had a private room set up so we could all enjoy dinner together to help her celebrate. It was a classy affair with a greasy little stripper dry humping the poor woman and the obligatory penis straws that we had to drink out of, but the food, at least, was great.

That was the best thing about New Orleans: the food. It was a gastronomic paradise. I couldn't get enough of the raw oysters, the po-boy sandwiches, and of course, the crawfish. And the best thing about these culinary delights was that they were all coming courtesy of the show by now. Everything tastes sweeter when it is free. It's like some immutable law of the universe.

After her party wrapped up, we were too wasted, so of course, we decided to head down to Bourbon Street to continue to get our drunk on. After all, we were celebrating!

Actually, it was worse than college, it was more like high school. People hung about in their little cliques. The producers would stay with the producers, the production team with production team, and the security team, well they were like flies on a shit heap, so they don't count.

YOU SNOOZE, YOU LOSE

My favorite night of drunken debauchery in New Orleans involved the male production manager who found himself unable to stand unassisted and needed the help of several security guards to make it back to the hotel.

He'd had a good night that involved losing a fight with a jukebox, though he did succeed in breaking the glass display and dirty dancing with four huge black hoochie mammas whose breasts were bigger than he was. That boy could grind. Of course, as the night rolled on and on he grew more and more belligerent. Hell, his belligerence seemed to increase inverse-proportionally to his ability to stand on his own two feet.

The guards tried to drag him back to the hotel while he did everything he possibly could to break free, determined to keep on drinking.

The guy was a poster boy for drunk and disorderly. It was a miracle he wasn't evicted from the hotel. Seriously. The guards bundled him into the elevator, and mid-fight he decided that he needed to take a piss, there and then. People tried to stop him but he wasn't about to be stopped. He dropped his pants and pissed all over the elevator, and being an ass, made sure he hit every button on the console, giggling about how everyone riding in the elevator tomorrow would have to touch his piss.

The guards barely managed to dodge the torrent of urine as he made damned sure he coated every wall before he dribbled dry.

Needless to say, he didn't arrive in the production office at the scheduled time the next day. We decided to let him sleep. When he did finally arrived, he stank to high heaven. I mean stank. He smelled like he'd been sleeping in his own shit and piss, on the streets, for a month. He lasted all of twenty minutes before crawling under the table he was using as a desk and falling asleep for the next few hours.

Shame prevented him from saying much all day, but he did apologize for the smell. He'd woken up in a pool of his own piss fragranced with a little vomit and topped off with a crust of diarrhea. It was not his finest hour.

The most significant aspect of this wasn't the bodily fluids, it was the excuse it gave everyone on the production staff. Thanks to his little snooze it became common practice for us to curl up under our desks for twenty minutes here and twenty minutes there, although generally we were able to wake up piss and vomit free.

TOO DRUNK TO CARE

During our time on the road a number of things began to niggle away at me. I'd had my doubts for a while, but stuff was beginning to come together and those doubts were festering into a genuine belief that this great 'search for a star' was rigged. And not merely rigged in the final stages but rigged from the auditions on, to the point that this entire charade was meaningless.

Two things stand out in my mind from the audition tour.

The first: representatives from 19 Entertainment manage the contestants while they are on the show. They traveled around with us when we were on the road and assisted with judging and all the sundry duties that went along with the auditions. I've already explained the 'truth' of the audition process and the rounds that each contestant had to navigate before making it to the final judging table where they'd face the actual judges.

The first time it happened I ignored it. The second time it happened I did a double take. The third time it happened I knew something stunk, and this time it wasn't our drunken sot of a production manager. I'm not sure why I noticed it. Maybe because for once I wasn't running around like a headless chicken so I had time to process and absorb what I'd just seen. But regardless, I'd seen it and processed it, and it didn't make sense in a good way. You see, representatives from 19 Entertainment were escorting individual contestants to the sign-in area, helping them sign up and get their paperwork and instructions for the final round of judging. By itself it wouldn't have set any alarm bells ringing, but all of the other contestants were either escorted by production assistants or followed the signs themselves.

Why the special interest in these few?

There were no straight answers to be had when I asked around, but I started hearing rumors about planted contestants and contestants that already had management and recording contracts... two and two makes four, right? Was that why these few were getting the special treatment? It'd bear some scrutiny, for sure. I mean, if they weren't special in some way why were the representatives from 19 paying so much interest in them? Why were they helping them through the audition process?

Our pal Occam returns. If it smells like a turd, and looks like a turd...

And this, this smelled like a huge steaming turd.

The second: it was in New Orleans that I really started to notice the significant amount of drugs and alcohol the producers were abusing throughout the audition process. Significant. That makes it sound almost sanitized instead of like a bad episode of The Wire. The producers were the ones who judged the open call – the first round of auditions – and after the open call the hopefuls would audition for Nigel and Ken, before getting to strut their stuff in front of the actual judges.

What I haven't mentioned is that if they made it that far and got to face the actual judges, the contestants were told to wear the exact same clothing, the exact same accessories, told not to cut or do anything else with their hair. They had to look exactly as they had done when they auditioned for the double act of Nigel and Ken. It's all part of the illusion of TV. The show would use footage from both rounds of the auditions so if there was something that stood out about the Nigel and Ken performance they would knit it together with the performance for the actual judges to create one seamless whole. Meaning the auditionees needed to look exactly the same. With me? Okay, back to the drugs and alcohol.

I'm no angel. I think we've established that, as well. I woke up on several mornings still hammered from the night before. Tylenol was my best friend on those days. Standard operating procedure for each city, but especially New Orleans, was to get the partying out of system during the first few nights so the alcohol was out of our systems before judging with the real judges began. I know I wasn't the only one to wake up drunk. Take the scuzz-bag producer who was cheating on his fiancée. He was a pill popper. We're talking serious addiction. I don't recall a single day on the road when he didn't appear to be completely fucked up.

And remember these were the same producers who were judging the contestants during the open call. Me, I was hidden away in the office working my drunk off. But no one ever seemed remotely concerned about this. But, and this is purely personal opinion, because taste is the one thing you really can't quantify, there were plenty of contestants I heard singing that should have made it through to the next phase of the judging process but didn't, generally, because their producer-judges were still drunk and impaired from the shenanigans of the night before. Face it, when you're drunk you can't focus and make accurate decisions. You're impaired. You can't drive. You think you can but thinking and doing are two very different animals. That's why the bartender's doing you a favor when he takes your keys. When you're hung over the last thing you want to do listen to noise, be it good or bad, and yet here you have thousands of singers taking turns trying their best to impress you. Your hearing is off, your vision is off, your mind is off, so riddle me this, how the hell can you make a decision about how well someone is singing and whether or not they should progress?

Hundreds if not thousands of potential contestants were turned away from the show because the producer that was supposed to evaluate their talent or lack of was either still drunk or wrestling a major hangover.

Fair? No. But whoever imagined this little dance under the spotlight was ever going to be about being fair?

CRASHING THE CLOWN CAR

During the Season 4 road trip, we acquired several 'voluntary' production assistants who took it upon themselves to travel around the country with us, working on their own dime. They would stay in hostels or at friend's houses and show up for work each and every morning.

As you can imagine, we're not talking about ordinary average Joe's here. These were social misfits who only served to add to the notion of the Idol tour being akin to a circus. They were our carny folk. They had nothing keeping them where they were, no ties, no responsibilities, no normal jobs or houses or anything, meaning they had nothing to be afraid of when we upped sticks and moved on to a new city.

I remember one guy we nicknamed Yanni – because no one knew his real name and he had that same wild look as the musician – always walked, staring at his feet. He had long dyed black hair but with an inch or so of light roots. You would have thought he was mute, he talked so infrequently. And there were two girls that traveled with us, one was pretty with a lip piercing while her friend was cursed with the face of a troll doll (you know the ones, you were supposed to blow on their hair and make a wish. They were ugly little things that were popular in the 1990's.) For the double-whammy she had a voice that fell somewhere between Roseanne Barr, and Fran Drescher's New Jersey drawl. We're talking nails dragging down chalkboard intonations. Of course that damned voice of hers earned her the job of wrangling the line of contestants. She'd clamber up onto a perch and holler her announcements into a megaphone for all to hear and tremble in dread as though before Zod or Ming the Merciless. These two went out of their way to try to make a good impression on everyone, hoping that we'd hired them to work the season in back in Los Angeles. You couldn't blame them or fault either their effort or their ingenuity. I know I keep saying it, but there are two sides to the Hollywood Dream, on the one side it's the fame, the talent, the stardom and all the trappings that go along with it, but on the other side you'll find the normal guys who could never be film stars or singers but who dearly wanted to live in that world. And Hollywood's equally capable of breaking both sets of hearts. Believe me. It's an equal opportunity dream shatterer.

Still, the full season 'hire-on' was the dream of most of the local production assistants we picked up to work on the road.

These girls were invariably the first ones on site and the last to leave. There was no way on God's earth they were sustaining those kind of hours without a little something to help them through the day. Trust me, I knew their duties and just how punishing they were. They were always on the go, and there was no downtime for them.

And it all came together to make a horrible kind of sense one afternoon when the troll doll was found slumped up against the wall in the production office, with what looked like foam frothing out of her mouth.

I dropped everything when I heard the call over the walkie-talkie. I didn't know what I could do to help, but I knew

I couldn't help where I was, so I rushed back to the production office.

I arrived as the on-site medic was checking her vitals. A crowd had gathered, gawkers rather than helpers in the main. I hunkered down beside the medic. She told me that she didn't think it was anything serious, most likely that troll doll had taken too many over the counter energy pills to help her stay awake.

It was a relief, obviously. They'd be fine. She was taken to the local hospital and had her stomach pumped and system flushed to get her feeling better as soon as she could. It obviously worked, she was back in action the following morning.

Right around then I found out Adderall Porn guy, my erstwhile production coordinator counterpart, was sleeping with both of them so at least he'd stopped masturbating himself to sleep. The girls basically moved in with him in his hotel room and stayed with him from city to city.

The caffeine pill overdose was nothing compared to what happened next with these two, though.

Somehow they acquired a vehicle and met us in the next city down the line.

Upon hearing about the car, both the production staff and the producers saw the opportunity to exploit them and their car in new and exciting ways, especially for interviews that they had planned on doing with contestants around the local area. It only seated five people, but rather like the old joke about putting Bob Marley in the ashtray they managed to get at least six employees in, if not more. Must have had a big ashtray is all I can say. Camera man, audio man, producers, and the driver.

They were headed out of town to do an interview when the car they had all piled into was t-boned by another driver who ran a red light.

Mercifully no one was killed, but they were all banged up and bruised, and obviously shaken. If I remember right a couple of them stayed in hospital overnight. They all returned to work during the next day or two, and continued to carry on as they did before the accident happened. Having been pressured by the show myself a time or two into doing things I really didn't want to do, I suspect they were feeling just as pressured to pile that many people into that cramped little car and drive around town. It was always the same thing, these local guys wanted to impress the people they thought could get them a job in Los Angeles. It's a high price to pay, if you ask me.

Sympathy was for the devil, and maybe a few of the full time crew that had traveled from L.A., it most certainly wasn't for the local hires. If any of them got hurt they were reminded that production assistants were a dime a dozen so they could either dust themselves off and get back to work, or someone would be happy to take their place. Everyone was expendable.

MONKEY SEE, MONKEY DO

Imitation is the sincerest form of flattery, right?

I made no bones about the fact that I wanted to become a production manager one day, so I watched what they did, and did likewise. Be it the drinks that they drank, the food that they ate, or the drugs that they took.

One of the much needed perks during that endless time on the road was that we were able to get free tickets to the *American Idol Live* tour that just happened to be in the same town at the same time we were holding auditions. We were all looking forward to the show because it was going to be a break from the normal grind of working hard and drinking harder. Of course, because they were comp tickets we had terrible seats high up in the upper left balcony area. Still, we were having a great time, the Idol's thanked us several times for all the hard work we'd put in last season, and most of us were up on our feet and dancing along with the songs, which of course pissed off the people behind us who had paid good money to see the concert: families with young children.

I've got plenty of sins etched onto my soul for when I meet my maker, and being a follower is one of them. Do not as you would do unto others, but do as the Producers and Production Managers did. I guess there were maybe twelve of us standing and dancing, meaning twelve people behind us, many of them under the age of ten. Unsurprisingly, the parents were asking us to sit down because we were blocking the kids' view. I heard the request each and every time but kept on dancing.

Eventually I made a show of telling others near me that we should probably sit down so the kids could enjoy the show but of course it fell on deaf ears.

Sometimes I hate myself.

Seriously.

Instead of just sitting down and leading by example I was more worried about pissing off the production managers, so if they weren't going to sit down, I sure as hell wasn't going to become the squeaky wheel. Call it peer pressure. Call it cowardice or lack of balls or just that whole people are morons thing, it doesn't matter what words you use, it's still a shit thing to do and a shittier way to behave when it comes to children. Let's face it, those kids were the reason we had jobs. It was those kids who adored the show. It was those kids who bought the records and tuned in week after week. It was those kids who had badgered and begged their parents to take them to see their idols. And we didn't have the common decency to sit down so they could enjoy the show.

I lost a lot of respects for the Idol employees that day.

I also lost a little bit of respect for myself.

I wanted to believe that I was better than that. That when push came to shove, I'd sit down. But I didn't. It was a sobering lesson to learn about myself.

She Crashed - Literally

The San Francisco auditions brought another big scare.

This time it was one of the hopefuls who'd sat outside for hours upon hours in the hopes that she'd be one of the first to get to audition. I remember seeing her there when we first arrived in the city. She was all by herself in line at the Cow Palace, where the auditions were being held. A portion of the main parking lot had been set up corral-style with a police barricade, just as it had in the other cities along the way. The barricades made the line easier to manage and prevented people from cutting in front of others. We had our opening production meeting, handed out assignments to the local production assistants hires, and we packed up to head back to the hotel for the night. She was still there at the curb.

Fast forward on to the day of the open call and everything seemed to be going just fine, we were coping with the huge crowds, no real crisis, and then, a couple hours into the day I received a call on the walkie-talkie: there had been a wreck in the parking lot and I needed to get out there as soon as possible.

My first thought was: christ, all of the contestants were lined up out there waiting to audition. I don't know what I expected, but worst case scenarios were flashing though my mind. I was breathing hard by the time I got outside. I raced out into the parking lot, looking frantically left and right for the crash. It took me a moment to register the junker that had crashed through the barricade. It was surrounded by security and other guys from the crew were rushing toward it.

I recognized her through the window: it was the same girl who'd been sitting outside for the last few days so desperate to be the first in line. She was slumped over the wheel, out cold.

The ambulance had arrived and the paramedics forced their way into the car to work on her.

The girl's body had gone into system-shock, basically, from neglect, lack of food, lack of water, and she had slumped into a coma. God knows what other medical aliments she had, but combined with the neglect her entire body just shut down. It was a miracle she didn't kill herself or anyone else, but by the grace of God the last contestant had gone inside just a few minutes prior to her starting her engine and plowing directly through the barricade. A couple of minutes earlier and we'd have been looking at body bags.

9/11 – AN ANNIVERSARY AND A HUG

Real life has a way of reminding us just how trivial stuff like a TV show really is.

My partner in crime, for instance, faced down a genuine nightmare during the September 11th terror attacks in New York City. They got the message that her brother, at ground zero during the rescue works when the second tower fell, had lost his life while trying to save others.

Mercifully it wasn't the case, and he showed up at his family's house, battered, bruised but very much alive.

Having made it through the hell of 9/11, one of his friends, another public servant, had decided to test his luck and bought a lottery ticket that day. It sounds like one of those apocryphal stories, but he won and we're talking won big, pocketing several million dollars. After the win he had relocated to Las Vegas, and as the tour rolled around to Vegas it just so happened we were in town on the anniversary of September 11th.

She needed to go see him. Not so much to say hello, I think, but more like she needed to share closeness with someone who had been there with her brother when they thought they'd lost him. I guess the date brought back all the dark memories and the fear. It's understandable. As a nation you just have to mention that date and we all remember with vivid clarity where we were, what we were doing, what we were thinking and going through, and for so many of us, it was a tragedy only as intimate as our television screens made it, so having someone there, thinking you'd lost them, yeah, I could understand that she needed some sort of closeness or connection with the guy.

I went with her, we did most things together at this point on the road.

After all the bullshit and the constant companionship of pretentious people, lackeys and lickspittles, watching them embrace, just standing there clinging on to each other, was a powerful reminder that everything we have, everything we cherish and love can be taken in an instant. I looked at them, hit by this huge emotional surge of gratitude for all the good days I'd had.

We didn't stay long. They shared some gentle chit-chat as they caught up, then we made our way back to the hotel to get ready for the night's events.

These few minutes of pure humanity, of peace and easy companionship, were by far the best few minutes of the entire audition tour.

THE WYLLEEN TRUCKING COMPANY

Back in the office after the seemingly endless audition tour, it was time to start to focus on Hollywood Week. It really didn't feel like all that long ago since we'd been put through the ringer by Season 3's Hollywood Week, and now here we were staring down Season 4's. There was never enough time in the day.

We worked unbelievable hours on the audition tour. My sleep patterns were shot. I was barely sleeping three or four hours a night. And far too often I wasn't managing even that. It was affecting my job. How could it not? I was still trying to be the Stepford Employee but this was killing me. It got so bad I felt the need to tell Wylleen, Jabba... why, I'm not entirely sure, but I had nightmares of just pitching forward face first into my desk, or worse, failing to turn up to work for the day because I'd crashed for twenty-four hours, Morpheus refusing to give me up from his tender embrace. And hell, sleep, deep, unbroken sleep, would have been heaven at that point.

I wish I could tell you now that her response came as any sort of surprise, but for all my sins, I'm a lousy liar. She rolled her eyes theatrically, let a world-weary sigh leak out between her blubbery lips, and managed a slow head-shake of disappointment as she told me, "If you can't handle the job and the duties that come along with it, then I'll be happy to replace you." It left a bitter taste in my mouth. I don't know why I had expected anything else, especially after the skin cancer scare. I was getting to see the same truth everyone else saw, get sick, miss a day or two from work, and you're out. That was the Idol way. So I did my job, but I felt like I had been hit by an eighteen wheeler long haul truck. In a way I had. Its name was Wylleen.

BUCK'S SPECIAL SAUCE

Everyone has their thresholds.

Me, I was growing more and more annoyed by the day with the abuse and the sheer amount of bullshit we all had to deal with. But I knew that no matter how much I wanted to let rip on any of the executives (including Wylleen, believe me brothers and sisters, including Wylleen) the satisfaction would be fleeting and I'd be out the door, bouncing on my ass down Hollywood Boulevard while they were scribbling my name on the blacklist.

Ah, the beloved blacklist....

Oft talked of, oft threatened.

I'm not sure if there really is a little list of Santa's not-so helpful elves, but I can well imagine there being one. Hollywood is full of shysters and schmucks and gossiping little queens, so even if they don't write it down, you can bet your bottom dollar word gets around.

I was threatened with the deadly blacklist on a semi-regular basis, but somehow I stuck around, moved up the career ladder adding new bits to my title, while Wylleen and the other executives bandied their threats about. Yeah, there's something a little odd about promoting a guy one day and threatening to blacklist him the next, right? Makes you think these guys are all schizophrenic, doesn't it?

You've probably glimpsed enough of my personality through these pages to realize I'm a bit of a loner, fairly aloof, and tend to just let shit roll off my back rather than stick, but this was getting out of control. In order to stay at least vaguely sane and keep my composure I needed to find an outlet. I needed to find something, no matter how insignificant, in which I could feel like I was getting some sort of revenge for all the shit, for all the abuse, but it had to be subtle. They couldn't know.

The first opportunity came along with a Starbucks run. There were no production assistants around. So I volunteered to head over to the Farmers Market behind CBS and fetch the frothy coffee they were jonesing for.

On the way back I noticed that the Farmers Market area had giant concrete planters that were used for landscaping. Something of a wicked scheme began to ferment in my mind. Call me Doctor Evil, but here was an opportunity...

I decided to stop at a planter and flavor the coffees with a little extra something. I stooped and scooped up a handful of dirt and continued on my way to the turnstile security gate that lead back onto the CBS grounds. Once inside the gates, and out of public view, I followed through with my dastardly deed. I had regularly suggested to the production assistants that we should start doing things like this to relieve our stress and get just a little of our own back on the bastards, but I doubt anyone ever went through with it. Put it this way, if they did they never told a soul, which in itself is understandable. It isn't like we'd all stick together. Anyway, I waited until I was inside the Studio's back entrance, which was always fairly deserted, and took off all the lids. I took pinches of dirt and rubbed them, grinding the soil between my thumb and index finger until the powder landed onto the top of each coffee like a sprinkling of chocolate before sinking down into the cup and dissolving.

Just for good measure I sprinkled copious amounts in each cup and gave them a couple of swirls with a wooden stirring stick.

I was literally in petty heaven when I delivered the coffees and watched them take their first sips thinking of all of the chemicals and processed cow shit and whatever else was in the dirt. I know this kind of thing happens all the time amongst disgruntled employees, and I was kind of proud that I'd done it, that I'd finally had enough of been taken advantage of and disrespected. In fact I was proud each and every time that I did it.

Since the majority of the bullshit came directly from Wylleen, she became the object of my affection. Every time I had the opportunity to do something like this to her, I did. If she ordered soup, I added my own 'special sauce' to it. If she ordered a sandwich or a bagel, I added my own 'condiment'. And I could be very creative. Gordon Ramsey would have been proud of my culinary inventiveness... actually, no, I think it was more akin to Baldrick's cappuccino in the trenches of Blackadder Goes Forth. Don't ask about the chocolate sprinkles.

Violence is never the answer, but there's something really satisfying about a little dirt here and cow shit there, with Buck's Special Sauce to make things go down a bit easier.

WELCOME TO DIVADOM

Around this time our beloved Adderall addicted porn loving production coordinator was out the door. Considering his many sins, there was no real reason for his sudden dismissal, but I wasn't going to complain. I jumped into the dead man's shoes and took over his role.

My duties at this point had increased to encompass looking after the production assistants, working with them on their day-to-day stuff and helping assign them to positions. The work was fine, but by now the contestants themselves were verging on the unbearable. Hollywood Week had arrived and those who'd made it that far were practicing for Divadom. They'd complain about anything and everything, no matter how trivial. First it would be that the craft service person didn't have a specific kind of tea they liked, or that they didn't have the right kind of clover based honey. Or or or. I'm sure they could sing, but their air of entitlement was seriously beginning to piss everyone off. But by now, of course, they'd had years to watch the show, to see how America reacted to the predecessors when they stood up to sing, and they'd bought into the fact that just by making it this far they were already stars.

PAULA'S WHITE CHOCOLATE FROU FROU

Still in charge of petty cash I knew it was not supposed to be spent on a bunch of frivolous things. During Hollywood Week the daily Starbucks runs were actually happening two and three times a day. I figured out a novel idea that would help the show save money.

Paula, by now, was fond of one of those frou frou white chocolate something or others. The production assistant with the arduous task of maintaining her ordered one the first day, no biggie, but when the second day rolled around she came to see me. Paula, it seemed, had only taken a couple of sips before pushing it aside. She wanted to know if she should waste money on another one.

I told her it was up to her, after all it wasn't my money, but don't skimp on the size, Paula wants a *venti*, get Paula a *venti* even if she barely swallows. The last thing we wanted was Paula throwing a temper tantrum on set because she didn't have enough white chocolate whatever it was. I'd made that mistake once on the auditions tour. Never again. I can still remember it with feverish clarity. I turned up with the coffee and she went off on me yelling and shrieking in that banshee wail that passes for a voice, the gist of the tirade being it wasn't a *venti*. Diva-style she demanded that we get her another one.

Of course the problem is when you tell someone a story like this they're pre-programmed to think you're having a laugh at their expensive, especially in an environment like Idol. So, I guess she wanted to test the veracity of my tale and decided to bring Paula a *tall*, which is just another way of saying the smallest cup known to Starbucks.

And true to form the poor girl was put very firmly in her place.

Champion of the underdog and initiate of Doctor Evil, I decided the coffee tyranny was just this side of pathetic. I mean, why the hell should someone have to suffer that kind of shit over a cup of fucking coffee? So, I took her aside and told her that there was no way we were going to let this lie. Instead, the new morning ritual would involve topping up yesterday's frou frou white chocolate whatsit with regular black coffee from the craft service table, and microwaving the day old, two day old, three day old, frou frou whatsit it until it was nice and hot, and delivering it as though fresh from the font of Starbucks.

There was never any risk of being rumbled. Paula is not the sharpest tool in the shed. The woman was invariably so loaded she never knew if she was coming or going, so the chances of her being able to tell week old white chocolate from fresh were negligible. And of course she continued to take her couple of sips a day as the coffee grew one week, two weeks, three weeks old.

PAULA CRIES ON MY SHOULDER

The food that the judges ate during any one day of Hollywood Week typically cost more than two or three production assistants would make for busting their hump.

The show would spend hundreds of dollars on food for each of them. During the actual lives show, Ryan's food alone would run between one hundred and one hundred and fifty dollars a day. And all he ate was raw fish! If there was a prize for the biggest whiner, Ryan would have scooped it every time. The boy was the epitome of a diva. Confession time: every time he pulled his shit I just wanted to take a crowbar and bust both of his knees. Does that make me a bad person? I suspect it does.

The amount of money the show wasted on gourmet food every day for those four could have fed a small African village for a month. The excess was sickening. You couldn't help but evolve a social conscience when you stared at the half-eaten Rabbit Food Paula would waste. And boy did she waste it. She barely ate but every day would order a ton of food. Just like the frou frou white chocolate whatsits, she'd take a couple bites then set it aside in favor of munching candy throughout the rest of the day.

The woman was an enigma wrapped in a conundrum smothered in mystery and frankly I couldn't be bothered trying to understand her. I don't think she was all that worth understanding. Mood swings, hysterics and tears.

There were plenty of tears.

I've had Paula Abdul crying on my shoulder.

How quickly the glamor fades. She didn't know who the hell I was, or what I was doing on the show, but that didn't stop her from grabbing my arm in the hallway near her dressing room, curling up and putting her head on my shoulder. Two seconds later she's breaking out into these gut-wrenching sobs and the tears are flowing as she unloads, telling me how tired she is, how absolutely drained, and how she just didn't have the energy to carry on with the show.

Paula cried on my shoulder at three separate times, for five to ten minutes each time. And then of course the next day was like any other, her memory wiped, she would never remembered me, nor the tears or the cuddles.

I could have pulled away. I could have just told her to get a grip, but I didn't, because it was pretty obvious that deep down she was just a sad person crying out for love. Hollywood's a pretty unloving place. You just have to look at the news to see the kids who come out here and end up as feature stories as a reward for wanting to be part of the freak show. It doesn't matter if it is someone like Corey Haim or Brittany Murphy, Heath Ledger or Michael Jackson, this place fucks you up, and it's been fucking up young minds for as long as it has been the heart of Dreamland. As long as there have been celebrities there's been tragedy. River Phoenix, Brad Renfro, Judy Garland, Lupe Vélez, Dana Plato, there's plenty of far too familiar names on the list of lives lost to the fame game.

So, hugging her and letting her cry on my shoulder became my good deed for the day.

PAULA'S SICK (AGAIN)

Picture this: judges, host, network executives, and executive producer's are heads down in a huddle, the buzz of conversation intense. Something was wrong. But this was Hollywood, fires were always waiting to be put out. I sat at my desk trying my best to eavesdrop without being seen to be listening in. Curiosity killed the cat and all that, and we've already established that I'm a nosy bastard, so it should come as no surprise that I listened in. It didn't take me long to realize the upcoming live show was what had their panties bunched. More mumbled words, not so happy sounding voices, and then someone said her name. Paula. She was the only one missing from the huddle. Maybe it was too early for her, or she didn't have enough coffee… or, and this was another case of Occam's Razor at its finest, maybe she was completely loaded up on prescription meds? If it walks like a drunk, squarks like a drunk and pops antidepressants like peanut M&Ms, odds are it's loaded one way or another.

Finally, she showed, loaded. It didn't take long for people's irritation to get the better of them. She acted as though she had ants in her pants and someone had coated her ass in honey. Up and down, up and down answering her phone—which was blessed with the loudest and single-most annoying ring signal I had ever heard in my life—and then there was the half dozen bathroom breaks during the two-hour meeting.

For the entirety of my tenure with the show there were rumors that she was going to be replaced. She was erratic going on neurotic with a splash of pathetic. Replacements were mooted fairly openly, the logic being she was so far out of it so often she'd be too strung out to notice, or care. Queen Latifah was the name on most lips. The producers thought she was the ideal candidate, save for one rather ethnic concern. She was black. The fact that she was black meant her addition to the judge's table would unbalance the very careful racial mix. Instead of white, mixed race, and black it would be white, black, and black. This, they thought, could be a problem as it would alienate much of Middle America.

Most of them, it seemed, were keen for Paula to be replaced. The level of the conversation dropped several decibels. The production team leaned in closer, all hush-hush and seemingly blind to the fact that I was sitting less than five feet away, making all of the cloak-and-dagger hands-covering-mouths talk redundant. The conversation shifted to the persistent rumors of her substance abuse. It wasn't really important what she was abusing, be it drink or drug related, something had to be behind her behavior. People just didn't act like that without some chemical assistance.

Point in fact, the show had received a slew of bad press already that season because of her. During the audition tour for the upcoming season, she'd turned up again and again slurring her words on live television and insisting she was a dancer—and while yes, centuries (in showbiz years, they're like dog years but shorter) before she had been a dancer, that had absolutely nothing to do with what she was doing now, nor how the show needed to sell her. She was there because of her voice. Shaking her aging booty was not on the agenda. I couldn't help but wonder if, in that addled head of hers she had decided the contestants on stage were all part of some dance off. Whatever, it was a little tragic. All she wanted to do during every interview she gave was dance. I guess the rhythm had finally gotten her. Of course, her people—did I mention the revolving door that was her personal retinue? PAs hired and fired on a monthly basis, no joke—explained away all of this odd behavior with the timeless classic Hollywood illness "exhaustion". Well opening bottle tops and pill boxes can be very tiring, I'm sure.

Of course there were good reasons for the gossip. There's no smoke without fire, as the old cliché goes. One of the benefits about not being top of the totem pole is that people talk to you, and those that don't talk to you treat you like you aren't there, so as the Invisible Man you end up hearing even more than you would have if they were talking to you. It's all very ironic when you think about it.

I'm thinking of one instance in particular, that started with her, late, on Jell-O legs, collapsing into her judge's chair. We were in St. Louis at the time. A production assistant asked for her Starbucks order and the best she could do was slur a few words back. The production assistant asked her again and again, like some hard-of-hearing comedy skit which only served to get her pissed. After thirty seconds of it, she pushed herself unsteadily out of her chair and fired off a volley of absolutely unintelligible filth—at least the security guard assumed it was filth, he couldn't actually decipher a single word of the rant—at the poor girl, who was only doing her job.

This, of course, caught the eye of the producers who were in the room finalizing the set up before opening up the door and allowing the auditions to start for the day. Well, it caught their ears first, but their eyes weren't far behind. They approached the security guard and demanded to know what in the hell was going on with her. It's not like he had to really explain himself. Everyone on set had seen this kind of behavior again and again, but of course they acted like it was the first time. Cue major shit fits. Unsurprisingly, tempers were lost—she had already delayed things by more than an hour at this point—and the execs and producers stepped aside to discuss the problem.

By now I was in the room. Being the show's coordinator I had to be right in the heart of everything. The delays already meant that lunch was going to be pushed back by at least an hour. That might not sound like a lot, but an hour would cost the show several thousand bucks in practical terms, and for every buck wasted the amount of shit I took from the head of production doubled.

I was always the fly on the wall in these situations.

I knew pretty much everything that was going on or that was going to be happening. I knew that the producers were pissed off, I knew the executives were fuming, but I also knew that Paula was rarely in a coherent state of mind. Scratch that. She was rarely coherent and calling it a state of mind was being generous. I spent the least amount of time with her allowed, and only then because I had to. I knew she was nuts and I didn't want to deal with it, but the execs had to spend hour after hour after hour with her. I almost pitied them. But there was no way they couldn't have known she was a walking train wreck 99% of the time.

I guess that's why she was had become our humorous punching bag. We made fun of her day after day, doing impressions of the way she slurred her words while one eye was crossing or just completely closed while giving a performance critique. And, of course, everyone from the janitors to the refreshments guys had fun with the way she loved to clap like a drunken – honking – seal.

But this, this was the mother of all train wrecks. She was still in her chair. That wasn't the problem. It might have been better if she wasn't. She had her hands folded in front of her and slumped forward with her forehead resting on them. I couldn't tell if she was even vaguely conscious. It was like watching one of those After School specials about drugs and the toll they can take on your body.

After delaying things for another thirty minutes and force feeding her cup after piping-hot cup of thick black coffee to sober her up, the execs finally made the call: she was in no fit state to go in front of the camera.

They sent her back to her room, and told her to sober up.

She managed to get back to her room.

Sobering up wasn't as easy.

When that audition show finally aired, she had almost no screen time, her comments cut down to nothing. And they still didn't make any kind of sense.

I guess she was really exhausted.

Of course, the official word was: she was "sick".

PAULA ON THE POT

Favorite is such a weird word when thinking about poop and Paula Abdul in the same breath, but my favorite Paula story during all of my years on the show has to do with the brown stuff.

Yes, poop. Poo. Number Two. Fecal matter.

I know, I know, I know...

But it's just too funny not to share.

So, the set-up: a film crew from the United Kingdom had come to Los Angeles to do a behind the scenes look at the show and the judges. You know, one of those fly on the wall documentaries about the phenomena that was Idol. I guess they felt some sort of ownership, given Simon's innate Englishness.

They were around for a week, and as seems to be the way in TV-land, the producer in charge of the whole shebang was this giant beast of a woman. Pound for pound, she gave Wylleen a run for her money. You get the picture, she was a big girl.

One of our production assistants was assigned to Brit duty for the week. He was at their beck and call, and I suspect, given the way they had him running around they were exacting some sort of revenge for Saratoga and the Boston Tea Party and all of those other times we spanked their asses or saved them.

I can't help it. It makes me laugh each time I think about it.

They needed Paula for some reason, a sound bite probably, something to add a little more veracity to their production, so he was sent to her dressing room. Paula was never one for answering the door on the first knock. Or second knock. Or third. So after hammering away on the door and getting no response—but knowing that she was in there—our intrepid production assistant slipped his key card in the lock and opened the dressing room door. The bathroom light was on but the door was closed so he knocked. God knows what was going through his mind. Maybe he had images of her lying on the rug, pill-popping froth foaming at her mouth. Like I said, God alone knows. But, of course, there was no answer. So he knocked again, and again there was answer. This little dance of knocks and no answer went on longer than was reasonable, so, worried, decided he didn't have a choice and opened the restroom door.

There was Paula, panties around her ankles, squatting on the toilet and staring at the wall.

She screamed when she saw him, started trying to cover herself up and just kept yelling for him to get out.

The poor bastard was traumatized.

All he could remember afterwards was the smell. As he so colorfully put it, Paula was dropping the kids off at the pool. I'm not sure the image of walking in on Paula Abdul taking a shit is covered by workman's comp, even if it scars you for life.

HELP WANTED: PAULA ABDUL

I never got the impression that Simon or Randy really liked Paula very much.

It's purely a feeling. I never heard them talking about her, but that's not surprising given that the few times I was fortunate enough to hear them talk the subject under discussion was either strippers or sex or strippers and sex.

I'm not going to invent some sordid tale of them spit-roasting some star-struck stripper, though I'm sure it would be comedy gold, but what I can tell you is they frequented strip clubs on a regular basis on the audition tour. Ryan joined them more often than not, which puts a perverse smile on my face. What can I say? I just find the notion of stripper boobs and stripper crotch in his face amusing.

Still, from what I saw, they seldom interacted with her. As my stay with the show progressed and my titles changed I had to spend more and more time with the judges and Ryan, but I didn't see any more interaction with Paula. What I did see was a lot of eye rolling between Simon and Randy whenever Paula was around.

And who could blame them? I mean, seriously, between you, me and these book covers, she was fucking unstable and that made her hard work. Crying one minute, laughing the next, then fast asleep with her hands folded and her head resting on them...

It's hard work being Paula Abdul.

I know you couldn't pay me enough to take the job, put it that way.

CAN SING, CAN DANCE, WILL BREAK DOWN

Hollywood Week, like every other Hollywood Week I'd lived through, was full of make-believe. The producers were working the angles, stirring up shit between the contestants who didn't know any better than to feed into it and sell the drama, giving the editorial suite plenty of stuff they could splice in during the final edit for the episode.

One contestant was fed so much bullshit by the producers that she broke down and fled the theater, running down the street into Downtown Los Angeles around dusk, which, believe me, ain't the best place in the world to be.

But the producers were relentless.

They scented blood.

Meaning they scented ratings.

She became their emotional punching bag.

They went after her like a pack of wolves stalking an injured deer.

I'd started to work out the way they did things by now. As well as the most talented, they went after the weakest individuals during the audition tour and purposely flew them out to Hollywood for the solely to feed the drama. It was all about 'good TV' remember, and nothing feeds the hungry audiences like the roadkill that is a broken contestant. Of course the show wants you to believe that you have the ultimate call, it's not so.

Why do you think each contestant auditions in front of Executive Producers?

It's not because they love the music and want to be a part of some great discovery. These are the ones who take notes on each contestant that's going to audition in front of the judges. They are the ones whose summary judgments are typed up night after night by the producers. And it is those notes, when it's time for the contestants to actually sing in front of the judges, that are printed so the judges can each have a copy. Forewarned is forearmed, right? Long before the contestant gets to warble a single note the judges are primed to know what to expect.

And those notes include more than just, can sing, can dance, looks good. They're all about how good a fit the contestant will be for the move onto Hollywood Week, meaning, sure, can sing, can dance, but it also means they're good for drama, weak or strong personality, can be manipulated, can be broken.

While the judging goes on the Executive Producers (Nigel and Ken during my stint on the show) sit right on the sidelines, just out of the camera's lens, allowing them to consult with the judges on any contestant.

These are just some of the things that you don't see on the show.

It's all cleverly manipulated.

And let's be honest, they loved the outlandish people because they made for good TV. So, I got very used to hearing the producers hyping up the contestants to be as outrageous as possible once they stepped through the door into the audition. If they could do the splits, they were encouraged to do the splits. If they had the urge to strip down to a bikini, they were told to do it.

Let's face it, you tell some wannabe with dreams of fame to cut loose and humiliate themselves and they'll do it if it means they've got a better chance of being on television. That's just the world we live in.

THE POT AND THE KETTLE

After Hollywood Week wrapped, Wylleen called me into her office.

She didn't like a couple of the people that we'd hired and she wanted me to make sure they never worked for the show again.

It's all about image. She didn't want fat or 'stupid looking' people.

It's a crock of shit. If you're a good worker you deserve the right to work. Who the fuck has the right to fire you based on your physical appearance? The goal, surely, is to have a great team of great workers. The days aren't easy. The stress levels are through the roof. So you want people you know are going to put a shift in. People you know are going to carry the burden and get the work done. But if Wylleen didn't like you, you were out. That's just the way it was, and if she didn't want them working on the show ever again, odds were they'd never work on the show again.

Now, we're talking a serious case of Pot and Kettle here, right? It's beyond ironic that Jabba the Cunt was telling me she didn't want fat people working on the show. Hello Kettle, you're fat, did you know that? Of course I did, Pot, but I run the show so fuck off and do what I tell you. Yes Kettle. Anything you say Kettle.

SOMETHING'S POKING THROUGH

You get plenty of colorful characters in TV, and very few of them make it in front of the cameras.

Easily the most 'colorful' during my entire stint with Idol started off as the show's receptionist. She left us to go to Fear Factor, and then came back to Idol as a production assistant.

First impressions: well, sometimes it's hard to actually say what your first impressions of someone are. One thing she told me was that back in her hometown she used to go into the radio station and do impressions of Demi Moore for the listeners. All I can say is that she was perfect for radio. If she was Demi Moore then I am Brad Pitt, Matt Damon and a little bit of George Clooney all rolled into a single perfect package of manliness. The only Demi Moore she looked like was a slutty chain-smoking ugly- stick smacked one.

Second impressions, then? Not that they're much gentler. The only thing that sticks out in my mind was her inordinate pride at the fact she'd had an abortion in high school, proud enough that she bragged about her late twenty-something beau and the aborted fetus during our first meeting. Obviously there was something psychologically wrong with the poor girl. Normal people don't blather about this kind of stuff to complete strangers, do they? Well, not in my world they don't, anyway.

What else can I remember about her? Breast obsessed. You know, I don't think I've ever met a woman who was more enamored of her own breasts, or the girls as she called them. She made a point of telling everyone she met—whether they asked or not—that they were real. Of course, that made them something of a rarity in Hollywoodland.

I got used to seeing her bent forward over one of the male producers desks giving them a show, or seeing her pinning them up against the wall playing tit-in-your-face. She relished the quick 'cop a feel' whether asked or ambushed. I think in some fucked up way she just liked the attention. It was hard not to feel sorry for her as the hands groped and squeezed, not so much because she had become meat, but because she needed to be seen that way. Your brain runs through all sorts of permutations when you meet someone like this. You start wondering what went wrong, what happened to them during their childhood. You wonder about what kind of family spawned such dysfunction. Was it down to being ignored or abused, or were they perfectly normal and perfectly loving and she was proof of nature over nurture?

She was also one of those frightening people who lacked a filter; what she thought came out of her mouth, whether the rest of the office needed to hear it or not.

I remember when Martha Stewart was in prison she'd ramble on about stuff like did Martha had a lover in prison? Did they bump pussies with the domestic goddess?

And when it came to her own pussy she would lean over conspiratorially and tell anyone in the vicinity that she shaved it bare and carried coconut scented wipes so she could 'fresh and zesty' whenever the whim took, which, on a strictly need to know basis, nobody needed to know. And then there was the whole bowel movement massacre.... nothing was held back. Nothing. The woman didn't have a subtle bone in her body. She'd regularly stand up and declare that something was poking through.

I still hear her in my nightmares: something's poking through! My sleeping mind turns it into an alien head, which makes the whole nightmare more entertaining, for sure.

COFFEE ROYALE

And then there were the drugs.

The usual lethal combo of pill popping and heavy drinking every night that seems to be a staple of the Hollywood diet. Bottles of wine during the week, shorts, shots and beer at the weekend. A couple lines of cocaine here and a few Xanax there. And it didn't hurt that her roommate (an illegal Green Card marriage guy) supported himself by selling drugs out of their apartment, or if times were tough, hanging out on the Venice Beach boardwalk. She had an endless—and free—supply of whatever she wanted, whenever she wanted it.

She made it abundantly clear that if anyone wanted anything, uppers, downers, inbetweeners, just to let her know and she'd take care of it. Plenty of employees took her up on her generous offer. By the time I left Idol, she was doing drug runs to her home almost as frequently as the Starbucks runs.

For all that, I never shied away from being her friend.

I enjoyed her company. She was a riot. Sometimes friends without that 'socially acceptable behavior filter' are exactly what you need to get you through the day, but I drew the line at being her drug-buddy. A drug-buddy's like a fuck-buddy but without the nudity most of the time. Sure we smoked some pot to loosen up now and then, but nothing harder.

One night, before a serious drinking session along the

Venice Beach strip, we were at her place with the drug dealing roommate, when she got a call from one of the crew asking if she could hook them up with a bag of coke. This whole thing was supposed to be super-secret hush-hush despite the fact that everyone and their aunt knew she was dealing, so she told him she'd come down and meet him on the street. I guess she figured Coke Boy would freak if he knew I was there. It's not like I couldn't look out of the window, though.

The guy who wanted the drugs was affiliated with 19 Entertainment (the management company that represented the contestants) and worked out of the Idol office on a regular basis. He'd always struck me as a decent guy. Put it this way, I had no idea he was a massive cokehead. Not that it particularly mattered one way or the other, mine is not to judge, so long as I'm not dragged into the whole mess. But here was this happy go lucky guy, married to a great women, living what seemed like a great life, it seemed a little sad that he was addicted to cocaine. I don't know, I guess it just graffitied all over my Norman Rockwell image of happy marriages.

Anyway, she was always trying to cajole other employees into doing stuff with her, not so much coke, usually it was pills. Prescription meds are like candy in Hollywood. Everyone knows it, but no one talks about it. And if she didn't have her candy she couldn't get through the day.

She regularly took advantage of the fact we were allowed to drink during work hours, going to the wine bar in the Farmers Market for a liquid lunch, and passing out on the couch in the back of the office for the afternoon.

She was a smart girl, it didn't take her long to cotton on to the fact that the show bought beer and wine on a regular basis, so she'd stash a bottle or two of wine somewhere in the office and, when the urge to imbibe hit, she'd grab one of the an extra Starbucks cups and fill that up, recap the lid and look like she was supping coffee all afternoon.

UNDRESSING ROOMS

And, as much as she loved to talk about her bowel movements and the drugs, her favorite topic of conversation was sex: the sex she had, and sex she wanted to have.

She'd meet someone at a bar and twenty minutes later she's be giving them a lap dance and shoving her tits in his face, winding the guy up just enough to be sure they left together.

As the weeks rolled on, her eveningwear slowly turned into her workwear.

More than once I nearly fell off my chair when confronted with her outfit of the day. There was the emerald green bra that she wore with a semi-sheer, very low cut (and we're talking about the girls jiggling around almost naked) white slip-on lingerie that had no right calling itself a dress.

And with that she would typically wear thong or bikini panties cut to give people an eyeful of her ass for good measure. I know, I know, I sound like a pervert remembering all of this stuff, but believe me, these images are burned into my retinas like a photographic negative and there's no expunging them.

She'd finish the ensemble with a pair of cowboy boots.

Sex to this girl was nothing more than another form of escape from the same demons that drove her to drink and drugs.

Sex and drugs make the Hollywood machine go around every bit as smoothly as money. The dressing rooms, for instance, weren't only for changing clothes. The show's male production manager would regularly borrow the dressing room key from me and have his girlfriend (who worked on another show across the hallway) meet there for a midday hook up. They were also the perfect rooms for a little cocaine to snort up flared nostrils, because of the privacy all of that prep work needed. Snorting a few white lines isn't as easy to disguise as popping a pill and washing it down with a glass of water.

I've got no idea how many guys she slept with over our time together on the show, which was hardly surprising given she frequently admitted she'd lost count, but I do know she managed to claim the scalp of at least one contestant and one senior Fox guy who just happened to be one of those supposedly happily married men you read about.

EATING DISORDERS

The contestants lived in fear of what Simon would say about their appearance.

I hadn't noticed at first, but it became blindingly obvious as Season 4 went on. I saw them eating, or rather not eating, far too often to be healthy. The female contestants would nibble here and nibble there, but not once did I see them really chow down. It didn't take long before the whispers started, and more than once I overheard someone saying it was because they didn't want Simon saying they'd packed on the pounds or mocking them during their performance.

I hated the guy for that – for making them feel so bad about their physical appearance that they'd starve themselves to please him.

There was plenty of talk during the season about the standout singer, and how she had acquired an eating disorder during her time with us. Her weight had changed so drastically in such a short time. While others were eating sandwiches for lunch she was nibbling on a salad leaf or a piece of fruit. I'm not going to sit here in the comfort of my armchair and berate any of them, or even blame them. I don't need to walk a mile in their shoes to know that no one in their right mind wants to be humiliated in front of millions of people because of their body. But this much I will say, more than once some of us crew members were concerned enough to discuss the issue amongst ourselves, trying to work out exactly what our moral duties were to these guys. Was it our job to ask them if they needed help? You could say it was, because we'd seen it time and again, we'd seen the stresses and strains take their toll, or you could say for a few bucks an hour, how could it possibly be our job? But then if it wasn't our job, maybe we had a moral obligation to try and help these guys if they were in need?

The truth of the matter is, as of today, no one has ever come out and admitted to having any sort of eating disorder while on the show, but admission and fact don't always go hand in hand. I saw enough, day-in, day-out, to know flat out that several of female and even a few male contestants radically changed their eating habits during their time on Idol. That's undeniable. It's also unhealthy.

THE POPE AND JERRY'S KIDS

In April of 2005 the office went on Pope Watch.

What is Pope Watch you ask?

What can I say? Get enough people in a room and sooner or later someone will run a book on just about anything. In this case we started taking bets on when Pope John Paul II would shuffle off this mortal coil.

The office television was turned on round the clock so we could watch the latest updates on his deteriorating health. Was it in bad taste? Oh, hell yes... erm, it's probably in bad taste to even use the word hell in a sentence so close to one mentioning His Holiness, as well, but me and bad taste, we go way back. I've made this excuse a dozen times already, justifying a lot of what I did on the show with wanting to fit in, wanting to be a part of the place, but just because it's an excuse doesn't mean it is any less true. I went along with many things that I didn't agree with because I wanted to stay on the good side of Wylleen and the others. So, when the betting began I placed my bet. When signs needed to be made and posted around the office so people could add their own bets to the pool, I was the one that volunteered to make them.

Since I was always one of the first to arrive in the morning, I was the guy that people came to for their Pope Watch update.

As you'd expect while the office was on Pope Watch, it seemed that all the jokes were focused around him and his health issues. Did he have a Holy Drool Cup attached to his lower jaw, did Stephan Hawkins (the man whose book effectively disproved the existence of God) let him borrow his computer voice to communicate his prayers to the Big Boss, that kind of thing. Most of them weren't funny, some of them were, I made a few, I laughed at more, and it was all in very bad taste.

But we were the same office that mocked the Jerry Lewis Telethon and it was shot on our stage in CBS (but during the off season). Then the jokes and the jabs were focused on the disabled children who were involved with the telethon. Yep, we were a classy bunch. I'm wise enough to the ways of the world now to understand that everyone needs to make fun of someone in order to get through the day. There had to be someone who had it worse. Someone we didn't know, we didn't care about, and who wouldn't get hurt by our mocking, because they'd never know about it. There's an abject lesson in humanity in this story, I think. I know the term is supposed to be 'object' but 'abject' just seems more fitting.

HOBSON'S CHOICE

Towards the end of Season 4, I was given a choice by Wylleen.

It was what they call a Hobson's Choice—a free choice in which only one real option is offered. Think Catch-22, Morton's Fork, a double bind. Mine was:

Either I work on another one of her shows and not got home to visit my family for a couple weeks over the summer or I don't take the job, go home to visit the family, and then return to Los Angeles unemployed. Tis the classic Hobson's Choice. Have a job or don't. Make no bones about it; I was blackmailed into taking her extra job because my job on Idol was threatened.

I hated the fact that I was being threatened, but what I hated even more was the fact she was forcing me to choose between my family and my job.

My dad's health was rapidly declining by this point and no one knew how much longer he would be around. All that we did know was that his time was finite. There wouldn't be many more opportunities to spend time together. So you tell me, what kind of choice is it?

It killed me, I mean it tore my insides apart, but for some stupid reason I couldn't bring myself to break down and show my feelings to my family when I called, so I bottled everything up and told them the truth, that I'd been given the choice of visiting them and losing my job, or staying, working my ass off on some extra job, and keeping my real job.

What were they going to say?

Of course they said, "Stay and work and we'll see you around the Holidays."

The thing is family should come first.

Dad should have come first.

But I needed my job and will always have to live with the fact that when push came to shove I chose work.

Because of this new job, I wasn't around the last few weeks of the season and I missed the finale.

HANGING BY A THREAD

A rigger working on the lights above the stage fell.

The stage was several stories tall, the lights around the stage were several feet off the floor. The only way for the riggers to get around from light to light was by walking on these narrow pathways between them. The pathways had short railings on either side that aren't much when it comes to life and death safety.

After the accident I was told that, because of the risks involved, it's common for at least two riggers to work the same job in case something goes wrong.

I'd seen how cheap the show was in other areas, so I wouldn't have been surprised if the lack of that second rigger helping out was due to the show's budget constraints. I'd also seen firsthand how corners got cut, even when safety was involved.

Since the show wasn't live and nothing was happening on or around the stage it was the ideal time to fix lighting problems and those other technical jobs that needed to be done.

I'm going to guess that no one knew he was on the set doing his fixes, because if they had known I'm hoping the guy wouldn't have hung upside down for as long as he did.

Yeah, the daring young man on the flying trapeze hung there, upside down, dozens of feet from the ground.

The guy had slipped while walking along one of those narrow pathways. Thank God he had been wearing the proper safety gear, so the safety cord caught him there, suspended above the stage. He could have been screaming himself hoarse, it wouldn't have helped. The stage is sound proofed. In CBS no one can hear you scream.

By chance, someone from CBS found him when they did the trash can rounds. If they hadn't, he could have been up there all night.

He tore open his leg during the fall.

While he hung upside down the blood ran down his body and over his face and dripped down through his hair to puddle on the stage.

I arrived when the paramedics were wheeling him out. You've heard that phrase 'as pale as a ghost'? He was. Believe me. I'd always thought it was a dumb cliché, but this guy was a color I wouldn't have thought possible. It was two shades beyond ashen. I've got no idea how long he hung there. I don't think he knew, for that matter. I think time loses a lot of meaning when you're hanging on by a thread—or in this case a safety cord.

TOKING AND FARTING

It gets to a stage when it all becomes very boring and very predictable.

It was like that with the drugs.

Season 4 was like Season 3 was like Season 2.

As coordinator, it was my duty to watch over the contestants, and given the way a year or so prior I had been driving them around Los Angeles stoned out of my mind, it was rather a turnabout. With great power comes great responsibility, as Stan Lee's web-slinging hero learns fairly early on in his super hero life. Well, I only had half of the equation, which is probably why I didn't feel so super. It didn't take a lot of overseeing to realize that some of the production assistants were more suited to office duties while others were doing us all a favor by being out, driving all around Los Angeles on errands. Knowing what I did, my first question before sending anyone out on a run was, "Are you stoned?"

I didn't care if they smoked pot. It wasn't my responsibility to keep them sober, but at the same time I took my actual responsibilities seriously, and sending someone out stoned and in charge of a fifteen passenger van was the very definition of irresponsible.

I think everyone who starts working in television is sworn to take the Hypocrites Oath. You know the one: do as I say, not as I do. I was still toking on my joints and drinking, but I wasn't in charge of a moving vehicle and fifteen other lives. By now you're probably reaching the conclusion that I'm an ass. Putting all this stuff down on paper I'm beginning to wonder the same thing and there's only so many times I can say "But everyone else was doing it," and not come across like some spineless dickwad. The truth is I did plenty of stuff I am not proud of but I own my own actions now. I know what I did, I know why I did it, and though that doesn't excuse it, better people than me have spent years and paid thousands in therapy bills to come to that level of self-awareness. I'm a better man now than I was, but I am still a long way from perfect and I don't see the point in candy coating these recollections from my days on the show. When I fucked up, I fucked up. I own those fuck-ups. I'm not hiding from them now.

Okay, so, one of the production assistants had an empty cargo van (think Scooby Doo's Mystery Machine) that he used as his personal vehicle. It wasn't uncommon for us to load into the van, close all the doors and windows, and hot box the entire vehicle passing around two or three pipes or joints at any given time. It was like we had driven back to the Summer of Love, man. Okay, bad hippy voice off. The stench would linger on us for the rest of the day, but I had a cunning plan for masking the smell when I returned to my desk, which, remember was located right outside of Wylleen's office. I was never one to disguise the fact that when I needed to fart I let it rip. Here's my philosophy: when you have to go, you have to go. Deep, aren't I? But let's face it, it really isn't worth trying to hold it in and get a stomach ache or make yourself uncomfortable when you've got to be in the office for twelve, fourteen, sixteen, even twenty hours. I invested in a bottle of Glade scented air freshener and kept it beside the phone. This was all thought out, planned even to the point of deviousness. Whenever I had to fart I would just give the can a quick shake squeeze one off to perfume the other one I'd just squeezed off. But Glade scented air freshener is also the ultimate weed masker. Fake a fart or force a fart, then Glade away all of that incriminating evidence. What can I say? I could have been a criminal mastermind.

VOTEFORTHEWORST.COM

The website VoteForTheWorst.com came up in discussions regularly during Season 4.

You know the place, right?

It's an anti-Idol website basically.

They pick the worst male and worst female contestant and encourage viewers to vote for the worst. There's lot of talk, mailbags full of letters from folks about the performances, and none of them are good. So, if you didn't know, now you know. Check it out. I love VoteForTheWorst.com.

The producers spent way too much time cruising around that website during the day.

They were obsessed with it.

Seriously.

That whole notion of 'don't read your own press because that way lies madness', forget it. They would sit in the editing bays during breaks and see what the latest talk on the boards was. The contestant coordinator, whose desk was next to mine, would spend hours on the site reading comment after comment. Again and again I'd hear people calling it bullshit and declaring it wouldn't last much longer (but as of today it's still there lobbying for *American Idol* 9 contestants Tim Urban and Paige Miles, so obviously it didn't last... oh, erm, I guess it did), and for all the talk of not listening to negative press and not paying attention to haters, it was pretty damned obvious that VoteForTheWorst.com had made an impression at Idol HQ. But that is the whole Internet culture right? You claim it means nothing, is unimportant, irrelevant, and yet stare at it and obsess over it and keep returning to the scene of the train-wreck over and over again whilst saying loudly, "It's bullshit, ignore it."

If it doesn't mean anything, if it is bullshit, then why spend so much time and energy obsessing over it?

Of course what I love most about VoteForTheWorst.com is the fact that the guy running the place is absolutely fearless in the face of threats and intimidation from Idol and FremantleMedia.

He understands what freedom of speech is all about in this modern wired-up world and good luck to him.

THE NEW GUY

As I've already mentioned, Wylleen strong-armed me into working on that other show, meaning I missed the finale, but the minute I walked back into the office I was thrown back into the deep-end of prepping the Season 5 audition tour.

You'd think it would all have become routine by now, that well-oiled machine, but both production managers from Season 4 were gone, and it was like starting over yet again. One left because the show refused to pay her more money, which is hardly unusual in terms of reasons to quit. The other left because he got another job and a better position working on a Mark Burnett show. The guy they hired to come in was one giant douchebag. He was cocky, arrogant, but of course being married to a playboy model gave him plenty of reasons to believe his own press. If I had a relationship with a centerfold that didn't involve taking staples out, I suspect I'd have been unbearable, too.

He'd show up to the office with his pretty-boy looks, bedhead hair tousled and unkempt. Just like those jeans and t-shirts that cost the celebutards thousands of dollars for the privilege of looking like tramps, it probably took him hours and cost a small fortune for his locks to look as though he didn't spend any time on them. He was one of those guys who perched his designer sunglasses on the crown of his head.

He carefully cultivated his image, cruising up the studio on his motorcycle most days.

Of course, the major advantage he had over his predecessor was that he didn't fill my email inbox with hardcore porn, so score one for the carefully manicured man.

Alas, the new guy had no idea what the audition process entailed so I became his go-to guy for all things audition. I had to walk him (and the new security crew) through it and boy did it get very old, very quickly. I was used to having to stay late because as long as Nigel, Ken, or Wylleen were in the office the production staff had to stick around on the off chance they'd need something, and that would mean hanging around until around ten or eleven night after night, even though we were done and had squat to do ourselves. New guy was worse. The way he had it figured the production staff's lives should revolve around his schedule. Nice in theory, bullshit in practice. New guy would roll up around ten or eleven in the morning, when the rest of us had been in the office since around seven or eight, and stay on 'til ten or eleven at night to get his full twelve hour production time in. And I swear, just to kick us in the teeth, as we got closer to leaving for the audition tour he started spending more and more time in the office.

The longest day? Forget the Normandy Invasion, it was the seventeen hours I spent in the office with him.

But that paled in comparison to what was in store for the production staff when we hit the road.

PACK MULE

In order to save costs for the audition tour, Wylleen suggested the six production staff each take one of the giant red crates that were used the previous season with us from airport to airport and check it as though it was personal luggage. These things were close to five feet tall, square, and on wheels. Her reasoning behind asking us to lug these around airport after airport was that it was smarter to do it this way because they'd only count as one piece of luggage. Obviously the idea of us having personal luggage, say with clothes in, hadn't really occurred to Jabba. She didn't have the looks, or the brains. She really wasn't the whole package. When I pointed this out, it was recommended that we use a backpack for clothes for the next four months.

Of course, there's one born every minute, as the old truism goes: one of the guys hired to deal strictly with the production assistants did indeed leave Los Angeles with only the clothes on his back and the few pairs of shorts, t-shirts, underwear, and socks and the could jam into a small backpack. They were supposed to last him four months on the road.

I didn't need two suitcases, but that's beside the point. I wasn't a pack mule. Four months on the road is uncomfortable enough, trying to coordinate laundry for the entire crew, juggling all of the ever-expanding duties, and all this bright idea of Wylleen's promised was more grief during an already stressful time. No thanks.

THE KIT FEE

I was tired by now. Very tired. Bone tired. Even before we left I'd started giving serious thought to looking for another job. It was only a nebulous *'I'm tired I don't want to do this forever'* sort of thought. I hadn't drawn any lines in the sand yet, but that soon changed.

It's typical that production managers, coordinators, and craft services employees received a "Kit Fee". A kit fee is basically a weekly dollar amount that you're paid by the show, tax free, for using your own equipment for work purposes. If you'd got your own personal laptop that you used for work purposes, you'd receive a kit fee, just the same way that if the person in charge of craft services used their own equipment (serving trays, utensils, coffee makers and such) to cater the show would.

The new production manager was receiving a kit fee for his personal computer, so given the fact that I was one of two people essentially running the entire production side of the audition tour, I figured that I was more than entitled to a kit fee of my own. I had bought a brand new Apple from the store in The Grove shopping area directly behind the CBS studio. I checked my eligibility for the kit fee with the production manager and was told that I qualified for the kit fee because of my title and responsibility on the tour, so I set up a meeting with Wylleen to get her to sign off on it. As with most things, she was in charge of saying yes or no.

Quel surprise she said no.

Her reasoning? I did not have enough responsibility on the show, nor enough experience to deserve one. So three nationwide tours, as in three more than the other guy, wasn't enough experience? And being one of the two people in charge of running the entire production side of the circus wasn't enough responsibility?

I was done. Any loyalty I had to the show went out the window in a hot wet sticky fart. It was a joke. One for all and all for one became look out for number one. So I started looking out for number one the best way I knew how. I spent their money on my personal needs; drinking, drugs, food, the works. Whatever I needed, they paid for. Instead of spending my hard earned money, I grabbed extra taxi receipts to cover my ass. Hanging around with the bosses on Season 4 had taught me well.

THE NERVOUS DRUG MULE

They might not have done it before, but I had, and given the new guy's intensity, I just had a gut feeling that this time surviving the road was going to be harder than before.

My job was thinking ahead, planning, so I turned my expertise on myself and decided it'd be fairly smart to fix some muscle relaxers or Vicodin to take at night. Given the dearth of downtime, I was going to need to sleep pretty much as soon as my head hit the pillow. I could have easily scored from the drug addicted office slut, but I also knew that in doing so it would be approximately five minutes before the rest of the office knew so I decided to buy them from the former production manager who had begun working across the hallway on another show.

I called him on his extension and met him in the hallway to do the exchange. Money traded hands. And I collected the pills from the backseat of his car. I went with the Vicodin as I figured I could more than likely talk myself out of any trouble with them at the airport. I had prescriptions at home that looked very similar. My plan was to just switch the bottles.

Imagining full cavity searches and other human rights violations, I was absolutely scared shitless once I arrived at the airport. I mean, I must have ticked off a dozen no-fly warning signs with the sweat and the shifty eyes and the shifting from foot to foot and not making eye contact and all of the other dumb shit nerves had me doing.

It took forever to get a grip on myself, but when I did, I realized that I was being a moron. The pills were checked in with my baggage, not carry-on. No one was going to empty my case and palm out individual pills to see they matched the label on the pill box, and so I added another string to my bow, drug mule.

BUYING OFFICE SUPPLIES (AGAIN)

Things had gotten to the point that during Season 5 I actually began to relish things going wrong. Hand on heart, I laughed to myself each and every time fecal matter hit the fan. I came to love going to the airports and checking in those red crates because nine times out of ten they were well over the one hundred pound weight limit, which meant that we would have to dump as much as we possibly could to make the weight limit. The amount of money that was just thrown in the trash at airport after airport was staggering. Two, three, four times the amount of money it would have cost to ship the damn crates went into the trash.

Like I said, Wylleen wasn't blessed with the smarts.

We spent so much money making copies of the legal paperwork, auditions rules, releases, ticket confirmations, and we just kept on copying them from city to city, wiping out some stretch of tropical rainforest somewhere in the name of Hollywood Dreams. Trees be damned, I loved it when they weighed each crate, sucked in a deep breath and shook their heads slowly like a car mechanic and said we were ten, twenty, thirty, forty pounds overweight.

At first it was just paperwork, but as time went by we had to start throwing away staplers, paperclips, hole punches, tape, white out, scissors, reams of unused paper, and any other office supplies that weighed us down. This stuff quickly adds up in cost when you're buying them in every stop along the tour.

Of course it was only a matter of time before this came back to bite someone in the ass. Because I was handling petty cash and turning my receipts each week, the accountant wanted to know why the hell we were spending so much money on office supplies. It was so sweet to inform him that it was all down to Wylleen's genius and that because we were forced to cart the red crates round the country, checking them at each airport instead of shipping them FedEx, weight allowances meant we were having to throw stuff away every time we checked in.

But, in corporate speak this was spun by Wylleen into the following nugget of deflection: I was wasting hundreds of dollars a week because I didn't know how to purchase office supplies. Actually, I'd argue I was getting rather fucking good at it, because I was having to do it at least once a week. Go figure.

LONELY OR JUST PLAIN MEAN?

As soon as we touched down on the tarmac of city number one I knew we were in for a clusterfuck of a tour. By then Murphy was our road manager. You know Murphy, they named the Law after him: what can go wrong will go wrong. We're talking chaos. Not nice organized chaos like the Mandelbrot set. Proper chaos. And it was made worse by the fact that unlike previous years, the audition tour was so big we had to return to each city, doubling the logistical complexity of things and the time away from home. I really wasn't looking forward to four months of it. The entire tone was set within a couple of minutes of arriving at hotel number one when a fight broke out between the producers and the guy hired to deal with the production assistants. It wasn't pretty, people were threatened, but as with a lot of those hot-air blusters no actual swings were taken. They came later.

Another change from the previous season's tour was that we had no time off or breaks, because we had to cram in twice as many stops on the road everything was jammed together back to back to back to back. We would essentially be working eight days a week, yeah okay, it wasn't that bad. The producers hadn't worked out how to manipulate the time space continuum. The schedule had "days off" inked in, but in practice those days off ended up being worked because the new production manager was so unsure of himself that he made everyone on the production side of things work whenever he worked, regardless of if there was any work for them to do.

His mantra was, if he was working, we were working.

This was fine for the first week or so, but as the days added up it began to get out of hand. He would guilt us and if guilt didn't work, threaten us. A common threat involved our being replaced and stranded in whatever city we were in if we didn't stay with him. It really didn't matter if we had work to do, or if we were twiddling our thumbs or sticking them up our collective asses. Maybe he was afraid of the dark? Or maybe he had abandonment issues? He certainly didn't want to be left alone.

I remember his wife's visits vividly. She'd catch up with us on the road every so often and was always so furious with the way he had transformed us into slaves who couldn't do anything unless we got his permission first. More than once I saw her screaming at him because of the ridiculousness of it: we were all crowded into his room, we lay on the bed doing nothing while he worked on his computer. She couldn't understand why he felt the need to essentially hold us hostage.

After she battered him into allowing us to leave the hotel, we stepped out into the late afternoon San Francisco air, hoping to see some of the city. It felt great to get out from the dark and dingy hotels and sweaty stale production offices we'd been living in. We were dreaming of a decent lunch, a couple of hours of downtime and bullshit to help relieve stress that had slowly but surely built up inside us over the week.

Less than fifteen minutes after we walked out of the hotel lobby my phone rang.

I knew it was him before I answered.

"I need you all back here, now. Bring our red crates to my room. We've got to do inventory. I need to know how many of each item we've got."

There was no point to this at all, remember we bought and threw away the red crate items in every city.

The guy, for all his smooth good looks and his designer shades and cocky walk, was, deep down, I thought, so insecure he needed one of us there at all times to offer a second opinion. Thank god making a TV show isn't open heart surgery or we'd have all coded in San Francisco.

Sometimes I don't judge people right. I mistake insecurity for cold-blooded bastardishness. The guy didn't want us there for a second opinion, he wanted us there for when things went wrong so we, and especially me, could be thrown under the bus to save his worthless ass.

A THREE-POINTER FROM THE FOUL LINE

There were a lot of peculiar relationships that started while we were on the road. People are predictable. By now I probably sound like some sort of misanthropic bastard, always moaning about who was getting it on with whom, where when how and every now and then, why. I'm not a prude. I don't really care which married man is fucking which married woman. They've got their own lives to fuck up as gloriously as they want to, or in some cases they've got open relationships where it's just fine and dandy to fuck whatever passing fancy needs itching at any given time. It's none of my business. But I'm not blind, when the production manager and the assistant to one of the executive producers start getting down and dirty eyebrows are going to rise.

Sure, no one really knows what goes on behind closed hotel doors, and if the downing went as far as doing the dirty, but innocent flirtation it was not.

While we were in Chicago the assistant rolled up the airport so beyond drunk that her breath was a fire hazard. Frankly, I was surprised that she made it through the airport screening. She was like a Weeble. She wobbled but she wouldn't fall down. Well not until she found a chair, and then she went down like Chasey Lain and in under a minute she was unconscious, drool dribbling out of her open mouth.

She was not the most useful employee on the road, and liked to party. This time she'd been lucky enough to hit an exclusive club that was the preferred haunt of a well-known basketball player. She'd scored herself a three pointer by all accounts.

The last I heard was that by the end of Season 5 the production manager's wife had filed for divorce. Draw your own conclusions, if you will.

SMOKELESS ASHTRAYS AND LOTION

So what was the most essential product we needed on the road? The one thing the show could not go on without?

A smokeless ashtray for Simon.

The man never followed the no-smoking regs inside hotels and the venues we hired. I don't know about you, but this kind of thing just irks me. I mean, it's plain disrespectful to people who've gone out their way to accommodate us, and nine times out of ten are working just as long, or longer, than we were. I don't know. Maybe it's just a pet peeve. Maybe there really should be one rule from them and one for us? Or maybe when you have enough money you just stop giving a shit?

And, apropos of money and just not giving a shit, one needless expense on the Season 5 road that left me gob-smacked arose when the head make-up girl (and the title head was something she took very seriously, if the rumors were on the money, if you catch my drift) asked me to send a production assistant to get Simon a certain type of lotion. She didn't know what it would cost, so I gave the production assistant a handful of cash to run the errand. Turns out that special lotion cost more than most production assistants would be making for the entire day's work.

After we wrapped for the day and were clearing out the

hair and make-up area, I found the lotion on one of the make-up tables, unopened. After all that, the damned thing had not even been opened. Well, waste not want not, as mom always used to say. I tossed it into my backpack and kept it for myself. If it was good enough for Simon's skin, I guessed it would be good enough for mine.

GOT A MINUTE? YOU'RE A JUDGE.

There were lots of things about the Season 5 audition tour that I didn't sit well with me. One was the fact that production assistants from Los Angeles were asked to go on the road with us. It just added unnecessary complications every step of the way. It was like marshaling school kids left right and center.

The Courtney Love of employees was one of the lucky ones who made the trip with us, but at least she kept things interesting. She was inches from being rushed into hospital at one point with a grand case of alcohol poisoning. I kind of liked the other production assistant until she started to sleep with a producer whose fiancée was in daily contact because she was planning their wedding. I know, I know, no judgments, let he who is without sin throw that bloody great rock and all of that, but happening again and again and again this stuff just starts to wear you down. People talk about the breakdown of society and the role of television in that, and seriously, they don't know the half of it.

This pair wasn't exactly discreet and were caught in compromising positions more than once, including one time when they were out in the hotel garden, her vamping it up as she posed very seductively for him while he snapped away with his camera.

We were still hiring local production assistants, so it really didn't make sense that we dragged Tweedledum and Tweedledumber around the country, but it wasn't my dime that was going down the drain.

The next twist in the sordid tale of Idolatry kicked in after a few weeks on the road when the L.A. production assistants were suddenly allowed to start judging the contestants during the open call.

Yup. It was bad enough that producers would show up hung over, and more often than not, still knock back the drinks while doing this, but now contestants were being judged by know-nothing production assistants? What skill sets or qualifications did these guys suddenly have to weed out the talent?

Seriously?

It was an absolute fucking joke.

They had no business judging the open call, they had no experience in judging anything beyond how long it should take to run a particular errand or how best to pack a particular box, and no reason to be placed at those tables judging talent.

It was a joke. Only worse, obviously, for the thousands upon thousands of people who came out to audition, because it wasn't.

Just think about how much money those hopefuls invested in coming to the open call, all of that time they invested hanging about waiting to be seen, because they mistakenly thought they were being judged by legit talent scouts who were part of the show.

So much for any dream will do.

I'm no saint, we've more than established that, but we were barely two cities into the tour and already I was finding it increasingly difficult to summon up the enthusiasm to keep buying into the lie that was *American Idol*.

I'd look at the faces of the kids lined up, kids that had traveled hundreds of miles and slept rough for God knows how many nights for their thirty seconds to hit the right note in front of the judges, and I started to feel guilty, like I was the one cheating them out of their dream. It was like a weight I suddenly started carrying around on my shoulders. I knew what was happening. I knew how the odds were stacked. I knew about the 19 guys escorting interesting auditionees; I knew about the Writers Guild-approved writer's scripting the reality; I knew about hoops keeping them away from the actual judges; I knew about the putative and punitive contractual clauses and so much more bullshit. And, of course, I knew what I'd seen in that elimination rehearsal.

It was hard to want to be a part of something that went out of its way to chew people up and spit them out.

BREAKING AND ENTERING ... THE MINI-BAR

I adored Austin. The city was by far and away the best stop on the tour, and not just because of the drunken revels and debauchery that took place every night, but because it was the first time on the entire junket we were actually able to enjoy ourselves.

Straight after unpacking in the hotel we headed to Stubbs and feasted. And I mean feasted. We gorged on food. A stomach full of food was a luxury. We'd grown used to the semi-starvation that came along with the production manager keeping us in captivity like giant pandas. That meant we didn't get a chance to eat properly and would end up going to sleep on an empty stomach. Who needs an alarm clock when your stomach is growling loud enough to wake the neighbors? If we were lucky there would be a convenience store near the hotel. 7-11 became my Mecca because, despite the inference of the 7 and the 11 they were usually open twenty-four hours a day and that meant we could grab a day old hoagie or a bag of chips to silence the beast.

I knew I'd lost weight, not that I was a big guy in the first place, but when I rolled back into Los Angeles one of the first things I did after sleeping for what felt like a week was to weigh myself. I've always weighed around a hundred and forty pounds, but when after the audition tour I weighed in at a measly one hundred and twenty two pounds. I'd lost eighteen or so pounds. I'd lost more than an eighth of my body weight on the road. And you could see it in the mirror. Standing five foot eight weighting a hundred and twenty two pounds made me look cadaverous. I lost most of my muscle mass and was reduced to malnourished skin and bones. I stood in front of the full- length mirror naked and was able to count each rib, but more fascinatingly I could see that I had eaten because the undigested mass had become an obvious distention in my belly.

The road had taken its toll physically and psychologically.

My diet had become so poor I would go four or five days between bowel movements, and was plagued by pounding headaches that would last days.

I really didn't like this thing that I had become, not the least because I didn't recognize myself inside the shell of a body.

The irony was, of course, that I was in charge of feeding everyone else, but because I was the production manager's co-joined twin, the logic was that I could get food whenever I wanted, but things have a habit of defying supposed logic. By the time I got close to the food most of it was gone and I was reduced scrapping dishes for scraps. I can remember one particularly desperate day I was reduced to eating a handful of butter pats. Just butter. I wised up though. I started stashing food like a foodaholic. I'd ram napkin-wrapped rolls into my backpack or pockets and scoff them down for dinner in my hotel room. Other stuff that I found lying around between meals, candy and cookies mainly, I stuffed into my mouth if I had the chance, invariably to the point of almost puking,

This didn't happen every day, thank God. But it happened too regularly.

Okay, that's a longwinded way of saying I loved Austin because Austin loved me. There were lots of reasons to love Austin, not least the amazing zombie flash mob that attacked the venue like something out of Shaun of the Dead but without the cricket bats. There were dozens of them, fifty, sixty, maybe more, dressed up like zombies that turned up during the first day of auditions and roamed around the venue moaning "Brains! Brains!" and causing chaos. It was brilliant. They were just completely fucking with everyone, and for that Austin will always have a little piece of my heart.

They left as quickly as they came, and as far as I could tell they didn't take any of the crew with them despite the fact that we had plenty of brain dead I would have been happy to lose to their horde.

Austin is a drinking city. And boy did we drink. Every night while we were in town regardless of how tired we were. We'd hit 6th street, where all the college kids went, and crank ourselves stupid. Stupid is as stupid does, right? That sounds like a Forest Gumpism. Forest would have loved us. In terms of stupid, one of our security guards got himself 'detained' by police for posing with one of the police horses, and one of the girls got so drunk her Coyote-Ugly, sexy dance ended when she fell off the bar. After liquoring up for the night we'd invariably make it back to hotel in time to splash dive into the hot tub and pool area for a night swims and drunken soaks.

And even when we were done partying in Austin and moved on to the next city Austin wasn't done with us.

I got a call from the show's travel coordinator back in Los Angeles.

There was a 'little' problem with a couple of rooms we'd vacated. Two rooms, the same little problem. Despite not accepting the keys to the minibars when they checked in, the fridges in both rooms had been broken into and emptied of everything. Given that one of the rooms had been occupied by our Coyote-Ugly dancer, and I'd met her in the corridors drinking wine at six or seven in the morning it really shouldn't have come as much of a surprise.

And speaking as not coming as a surprise, both of the rooms' occupants denied the smash and grab, over and over until they were blue in the face despite the fact that they'd been caught dead-to-rights. Some people just don't know when to shut up, but I guess being drunk on stolen minibar booze keeps the mouth lubricated.

THE CRACKING OF THE TRAVEL COORDINATOR

The travel coordinator and I were talking on a daily basis now. She'd entered at least the third or fourth circle of hell already, and it was only just getting started. She'd had to move into the office and was only getting to go home to collect her mail, shower and change clothes.

There was so much pressure on her it wasn't funny. She always had to try to get the cheapest flights and find ways to save money. Every time we spoke I could hear the misery in her voice, and it was getting worse and worse for each day we were out there. I've been calling it a circus, and to an extent it really was, all of these different acts, and all of these animals, and in the middle of it, the clowns. It was a miracle she managed to stick it out as long as she did, and it certainly shouldn't have been a surprise to anyone when she finally cracked, grabbed her purse and walked out of the office one day.

We were in Denver at the time coping with flooding hotel rooms, but that's a story for a different page.

Of course her exodus sparked a panic. Who was going to take over the travel duties? Someone needed to. We couldn't be left stranded on the road. It'd go beyond hair-pulling and into murder if someone didn't pick up her duties. The producer's first choice was Coyote Ugly, and boy was she against taking the job, but ultimately caved in and headed back to base to take over the reins. We had an impromptu going away party for her that involved copious bottles of wine and a veritable pharmacy of pills. In her honor I chased down half a dozen Vicodin with two bottles of red wine that night. Needless to say I had a blast but remember kids, don't do this at home, and don't mix pills and alcohol when in charge of video games as your judgment may be impaired, but at least everyone will get a laugh and you incompetence.

The moral of this story is there never has been one.

AND THEN CAME THE FLOOD

So, flooding hotel rooms...

As with Season 4, we'd picked up a handful of traveling production assistants who came back to Los Angeles to work during Hollywood Week. It might have looked conscientious on the surface, but what it told me was that they were desperate and would pretty much do anything to secure a job on the show for the upcoming season.

These guys generally stayed in the same room as our L.A. based female production assistant. Obviously that was a big no-no according to the show regs. Who knows what went on behind closed doors? Maybe it was simple fiscal expediency, maybe it was a reenactment of Sodom and Gomorrah. This bit is a little CSI, as no one really figured out exactly how the flooding happened, but you didn't need to be David Caruso to guess that the three of them had simultaneously passed out in the hotel room and left the water running in the bathtub, with the stopper in place. Who knows what is going through people's minds half the time? It didn't take long for the tub to overflow, and the water just kept on pouring, which flooded her room. Of course, they didn't wake up, so the flooding spread into the rooms on either side, and that whole 'water always looks for a way downhill' kicked in and the water seeped down into the rooms below, including a storage room where important files and other hotel related paperwork was stored.

The whole thing was an unmitigated disaster.

Miraculously, she wasn't fired but she lived in absolute fear of facing Wylleen when we returned.

DEPORTING BAT-SHIT CRAZY

The guy hired to oversee the production assistants had his South American girlfriend join us on the road. She traveled with us from city to city. To call her a handful was like calling the Son of Sam difficult to get along with. Not only was she a raging drunk, she was South-American-crazy, like she thought all of those bad racial stereotypes had to be lived up to. First it was temper tantrums in the middle of the production office because she wanted more attention, then judging from the noises coming from his hotel room, late at night, I guess she got it in the form of make-up sex. It was all a game to them, I think. Pout and shout and make-up. In the end we had to ban her from coming to the production office.

Not that the drama stopped once we got back to Los Angeles.

Some people live for it, I guess. It's not my idea of a life, but I'm sure there's some sort of appeal to having the cops turn up because your other half has gone batshit crazy. Answers on a postcard, please. Anyway, when the cops showed up, she bailed out of the second story window and landed badly in the landscaping below, scrambled around and stumbled into the road right in front of an oncoming car. It was like something out of a low-budget movie, and just to complete the picture in your mind, she was wearing the classic combo of panties and t-shirt. The driver slewed the car sideways, barely missing her and was rewarded for saving her life by an attempted car-jacking. He was too strong for her, and managed to hold her until the cops caught up with her.

SHE WAS HAULED OFF TO JAIL.

When she was sprung, her boyfriend figured it would be a good thing to take her home for a break, let her surround herself with her friends and family for a while and decompress. A sweet gesture right up until the moment they landed back in the United States, where she was detained by the police for deportation. What's it they say about you can never go home again? Well when Uncle Sam is sorting out your travel arrangements you sure as hell can.

LIGHTS OUT (TWICE)

Boston, Boston, Boston... how the hell do I describe Boston?
Let's go point by point:
There was the airplane scare.
I almost killed myself and over a dozen other people.
Two hotels lost all power.
And one of our guys wound up in the hospital after a serious fall.
Yeah, Boston.
Never a dull moment.
And we were only there for a few days. I guess we unwittingly triggered the Idol Curse or something.
We touched down, ate, did our on-site production meeting and returned to the hotel, so we're talking maybe three hours from our arrival in Boston, and the hotel lost all power. You've heard about the blind leading the blind? Well here it was us being led by flashlight up to our rooms to collect our belongings and being transported to another hotel closer to the airport.
Once is bad luck... twice is downright freaky.
They shuttled us over to the new hotel. We checked in and headed to our rooms to relax for the evening. We had to be up at 3am to drive over to the Patriots stadium for open call auditions the next day, so sleep was going to be precious.

While I was prepping for bed the hotel lost power.

Seriously.

Everything went out. The lights. The television. The constant background hum of the air-conditioning. The silence left behind was frightening. You could hear the wind against the windows and the old building creaking.

I panicked.

All I could think was that something was happening. Poltergeists or terrorists, and I really didn't like either alternative. It's easy to make fun of it now, but back then, in that room, alone in the dark, I honest to God thought we were in the middle of some sort of terror attack. Two hotels wiped out in two hours. They'd got into the Grid and were killing the power. We'd be defenseless without power. Blame the movies, blame 24, blame Jason Bourne, but my mind was racing. I was a mess as the hotel staff evacuated us.

It wouldn't have been so bad if people had just been able to tell us what was happening, but no one had a clue. It was close to midnight and the peasants were revolting because they were supposed to be up in a couple of hours. We stood there, arms wrapped around ourselves in the hotel parking lot, for what seemed like forever before we were allowed back inside and into our rooms.

And the entire time I kept scanning the horizon for the tell-tale orange glow of fire or something, anything, to explain why everywhere we went blackness was sure to follow.

Back upstairs, still spooked, I called my parents back in Oregon. I needed to hear a friendly voice. I told them what was going on, and like some character in a bad movie fed with dialogue like, "I've got no idea what is really going on. No one is telling us anything," tried to calm down.

It was comforting to hear their voices but part of me kept

coming up with these nightmare scenarios where I wouldn't be around when the sun came up.

Sometimes an imagination is a curse.

I locked myself in the bathroom. Don't ask me why. It isn't like tiles are the first line in terror-attack repellant, but it felt good to be able to see all four walls and for them to be close. I talked with my family for a while, not really paying attention to the time. It didn't matter what we talked about. I just wanted to hear another voice. I was close to tears for the entire conversation but whenever they threatened to well up, I wiped them away with my sleeve.

I made sure I told each of them that I loved them before I hung up.

I couldn't sleep. There wasn't much point. The alarm would go off in under two hours, so I stared at the ceiling with my arms crossed over my chest like Nosferatu in my coffin waiting to die or for the alarm ring.

TOO CLOSE FOR COMFORT (AGAIN)

Obviously I didn't die.

But the next day was hell just the same.

And I guess I wasn't the only drama queen on staff, either. We'd fed into each other's panic. People shared stories about how they laid on their beds and cried, others admitted that, like me, they had called loved ones in search of a comforting voice.

The reality of it, when all was said and done, was that we were all running on fumes and the open call portion of the audition process is never easy at the best of times. This was the worst of times. It was, without doubt the longest day of the entire week. It must have had twenty-eight or twenty-nine hours in it. Must have.

The new hotel was more than an hour away from the stadium, so of course we missed dinner.

The next morning I was given driving duties by the production manager.

It wasn't his best decision, having managed 5 hours of sleep in two days, but, with no idea where I was going, I grabbed the keys and jumped in the fifteen passenger van while the other employees piled in. I hadn't paid attention yesterday, using the extra hour in the car to try and squeeze in some shuteye, but there were directions in the van so I grabbed them and off we went.

Roughly ten minutes in the drive everyone else in the van was snoring and I was the only one even partially awake.

And that partially really was a grudging participant in the whole awake thing.

I couldn't turn the radio on though, because it would have woken everyone up, so I slapped myself across the face a few times, pinched my cheeks and basically tried to force myself to wake up properly.

I couldn't see the road signs or much else beyond the windshield. It was pitch black out there and streetlights aren't as common as they really ought to be.

It was like having a hypnotist as my co-pilot. I could feel my eyelids getting heavy, and in the back of my head I kept imaging the voice saying, "You are getting sleepy..."

I knew I was falling asleep, but the devil on my shoulder kept saying drive on and taunting me with images of the brand new asshole I'd be modeling if I woke people up, so, idiot that I am, I listened to the devil and did my best to keep my eyes open and all four wheels on the road.

Needless to say I failed, but luckily not spectacularly enough for once. We were on a straight stretch of road, well we were on it right up until the moment I put the van into the ditch and then jerked the wheel and dragged it back onto the road. While I didn't kill anyway, I did, however, succeed in waking everyone up rather rudely.

It was one of those horrible what-could-have-been moments. Even now, I can see it all unfold in front of me like some sort of black and white Bergman movie where Death's waiting with his chessboard.

During my doze I'd also managed to miss the exit as well as the ditch, and by the time everyone had dusted themselves off we were miles away from where we were supposed to be. Of course everyone was more pissed off by that than the fact I'd nearly killed them by falling asleep behind the wheel for the second time since I started working for the show.

People are morons.

Maybe it'd be third time lucky, I remember thinking, blackly, when none of them asked if I wanted one of them to relieve me behind the wheel.

If you take one thing from all of these stories, I hope it's this: the show demanded too much of people working on it. We were pushed and pushed and pushed beyond human endurance and into dangerous territory without thought for wellbeing. We weren't fed properly. We didn't get enough sleep. There was no feasible way we could have functioned fully.

This drive, and the what-might-have-been worst case scenario, has to go down as one of the scariest experiences of my life. The first time I fell asleep behind the wheel was bad, but then it had been just me. This time there were over a dozen other people in the van with me. Over a dozen people whose lives connected with dozens more people, and dozens more beyond them. Six Degrees of Separation from Kevin Bacon and all that.

And the echo of every other time someone spoke up about the wellbeing of the crew or the stress of the audition tour came back to silence me; I could hear Wylleen's voice telling me I had a choice, if I couldn't handle the job I was welcome to go, because there was always someone else who could. We were all easily replaceable. I wanted to write the word expendable there, but given the context the word just sent a cold shiver running down the ladder of my spine, I didn't.

And sometimes, when it's dark and I am alone, I find

myself wondering what if it had actually happened? What if I had survived? Would the show have supported me? Or if I had died along with them, would I have been blamed? After all, I would have been an easy scapegoat.

FLYING IS FOR THE BIRDS

Sometimes you don't need to shout to get everyone's attention. Sometimes you don't even need to say a lot, just a few words, and everyone will listen. It's as though something deep down inside us resonates to a certain frequency, attuned to those words.

We were coming in to land in Boston. The sky was smoky white, clouds thick and low-lying. There wasn't a speck of blue sky in sight.

It was the old woman in the row behind me that said the words no one wanted to hear and couldn't unhear once we had.

The captain announced that we were going to circle for a while to burn off fuel. The fog was making it difficult for the planes to land and no one wanted to take any risks bringing down a fully tanked up jet, so we were in a holding pattern along with several other planes.

I am a frequent flyer. Being up there doesn't worry me. I quite like looking out at the world below and seeing it in a very different way. The only time I'd ever been scared on a plane was when I was flying from Los Angeles to Oregon and we hit a massive patch of turbulence which caused the plane to plummet and shake violently. That was scary because it was unexpected, but in truth barely lasted ten seconds and then we were stabilizing. This was different. This time it was the anticipation that had me clenching my fists so tightly my chewed down fingernails dug into my palms so deeply I thought they were going to bleed.

It wasn't smooth, but I knew that was because we were in the cloud layer and it's always a little bumpy there. Looking out of the window was weird. White above, white below. I tried to read the SkyMall magazine, but there's only so many times you can thumb through the glossy ads before tossing it back in the seat pocket beside the airsick bag. Normally there's noise, at least more noise than the low engine hum, but this time the entire cabin was quiet. The quiet turned time to sludge.

And then the old woman in the row behind me spoke.

"I think I see a flock of birds."

They were her first words of the entire flight, and my stomach sank as though it had just hit its own pocket of turbulence.

A flock of birds.

How many times has a crash been explained away with: the plane hit a flock of birds, which caused the engine to stall?

I understand what they mean when they describe the rollercoaster as a white-knuckle ride now. I held on to the armrests so tightly it would have taken the jaws-of-life to pry my hands off.

I kept looking out of the window trying to see the birds.

Every now and then I'd catch a glimpse of something, but it was impossible to tell if it was avian or imaginary. And every time the engine hum changed, my heart skipped a beat. When the landing gear engaged I thought for sure birds had been sucked into the engine and it felt like we were going down at an alarming rate. And then we broke the cloud cover and were barely forty feet above the runway.

As we deplaned I looked back over my shoulder, out of the big plate glass window onto the hardstand, and up there in the sky, amid the thick banks of clouds, I could have sworn I could see hundreds of black speckles.

Birds.

Hitchcock would have been so proud.

Me, I bent down and kissed the ground like the Pope, so, so glad to be back down on it.

The Trip to the Hospital

One of the local guys that we hired in Boston was setting up the set for the judging.

I wasn't in the room where he was working, neither was the production manager at the time. One of the show's producers placed a call over the walkie-talkie saying that someone had fallen off a ladder and was lying on the floor. She thought that he'd hit his head on the way down and blacked out. Nothing about the message sounded good.

I jumped up from my makeshift desk and raced across to the judging room. He was still on the floor, surrounded by a handful of staff who were trying to help and not really doing very much. I put myself into the mix, asking if anyone had witnessed what had happened.

He'd been sitting on the ladder, straddling it, while he worked on something that required him to have both of his hands above his head. The next thing anyone knew he was on his back on the floor. He wasn't moving, but he was conscious. I've watched enough sports to realize people don't move much when they're really hurt.

It seemed like an eternity before the production manager finally made it into the room. We weren't medics. No one knew how hurt this guy really was. Christ, he could have broken his neck for all we knew. No one wanted to move him. I asked the production manager what he thought we should do and one of the first things that he said was, "Well whatever we do they're not going to like it back in office", referring to everyone who was back in Los Angeles. My first instinct was to punch him, my second was to call for help. Wondering about what the fuck they were going to think in L.A. wasn't anywhere on the list of things to think or feel that I had. It was obvious the guy had to go to the hospital. He wasn't saying much, but what he was saying was punctuated by pain.

I volunteered to go with him because someone needed to be there, but the production manager point blank said no, forbidding me from going.

That first instinct rose up again, pretty damned overpowering this time, but I curbed my temper. I couldn't believe he wanted to send the guy out alone to the hospital, I mean we're talking seriously cuntish behavior, and this once, finally, I stood my ground. I didn't care what the idiot said, I was going to take the guy to hospital and make sure that he was okay.

In a truly dazzling moment of humanity the production manager came out with a gem, not only was he more worried about the show being thrown off schedule than he was about the guy, he happily informed me that if anything whatsoever went wrong while I was gone I was the one taking the blame, not him. The lack of compassion shouldn't have surprised me, but it did. And it was that surprise coupled with pure bloody anger that made me stand my ground.

I had a production assistant drive us there in one of the vans.

We'd barely walked into the ER when my phone started ringing.

It was the Los Angeles office, meaning it was Wylleen. The

questions were short and sharp: what happened, does he need surgery, if so, does he have to get it there. It took me a moment to realize that the questions weren't grounded in concern for the guy but rather concern at the cost and how much money the show was going to have to pay out because it was a workplace injury.

It felt as though I was on the phone the entire time.

I don't really remember the guy being taken into be examined or anything else for that matter.

I am happy to say that he was lucky and walked with an arm in a sling and some bumps and bruises. There was no head trauma and his spine was fine.

Not one person asked how he was when I got back to the venue.

THE ASIAN BIRD FLU?

I began to think we really were cursed when it came to airplanes during the Denver to San Francisco leg of the tour.

We were on the hardstand ready to depart.

A lady towards the rear of the plane was complaining about how she felt sick and didn't want the flight to take off because of way she was feeling, she was too sick to fly, but at the same time she didn't want to get off the plane.

Now a little perspective to this: the main news item of the week was the Asian Bird Flu and there she was, just a few rows behind me when I glanced back to see what all the fuss was about. She didn't look good. She was sweating and obviously in considerable discomfort. Couple that with the fact that she was Asian, which by itself was enough to kindle at least a little irrational paranoia, and had just arrived back in the States after visiting her family in Asia. She told the attendants she had begun to feel ill before she boarded her flight to the United States.

You could see the flight attendants were starting to get worried.

They would huddle up together for a few seconds, whisper, and then turn around and go their separate ways.

We were delayed almost an hour already.

One of the flight attendants took up her post behind my

seat. After maybe twenty more minutes I finally turned around and asked her what was happening.

She told me it was nothing to worry about and that we would soon be taking off.

I told her that I didn't think it was reasonable for them to expect any of us on the flight to ignore what was going on. The woman had just returned from Asia and was complaining about being violently ill, sweating profusely while sitting in her seat. It wasn't scaremongering. It was worrying. I suggested it might be a good idea to make some sort of announcement about what was going on and why we hadn't taken off yet. She didn't agree.

This went on for at least another thirty minutes or so before police officers entered the plane and forcibly removed the woman from the flight.

As she was escorted off the plane she removed her coat. The back of her neck was raw and red with weeping lesions, and several patches of skin on her arms appeared to be weeping pus.

The whole way to San Francisco I kept thinking about the recycled air we were breathing through the pressurized cabin and about the weeping sores and Asian Bird Flu, trying to remember what, exactly, the symptoms were and just how contagious it was supposed to be, all the while remembering how many times I'd heard people say they'd caught the sniffles off someone on a plane.

I was barely through the Gate before I started placing calls to the airline and when that failed to offer any answers, the Center of Disease Control. I'll make no bones about it, I wanted to know if we'd been exposed to Bird Flu or any other type of contagion because of this woman.

A dozen calls yielded zero answers.

I finally gave up and figured that if I started to sweat or felt lesions forming on my neck, then I'd worry. By which time, of course, I would have more likely than not contaminated the greater part of San Francisco thanks to the thousands of people turning up to audition. We'd already brought a zombie infestation out in Austin, maybe we could go the whole hog and bring the plague to San Francisco?

CELEBRITY GOSSIP

While on the road, our only real method of escape was the computer.

I've always found the notion of Celebrity fascinating. I'm one of these guys who scours the gossip sites devouring anything and everything Hollywood. I bought Star Magazine and perused the tabloids, so naturally any free time I found would be traded in for the column inches of the gossip blogs.

My two favorites at the time were Perez Hilton and Dlisted.com.

I liked the snarky, smack-talking sarcasm.

I still read both of those blogs on a daily basis, but I've added Radar Online and TMZ.com to the mix a well.

DOWN FOR THE COUNT

Greensboro was an interesting place, and completely unexpected at that.

When it was announced that the audition tour would be making a scheduled stop in Greensboro, most of us figured the higher ups had suffered some sort of collective brain fart. Hell, most of us didn't have a clue where Greensboro was.

You'll recall I wanted to thump the production manager not so long ago. Well, as it turns out I wasn't the only one. Come Greensboro, come the Clash of the Titans. We're talking the Thriller in Manila. We're talking... well, okay, not to go all Don King on you, but we roll into Greensboro and all hell breaks loose between the production manager and one of the producers. This thing was epic.

Sure I was biased, sure I wanted to be doing the thumping, the pounding, delivering the beat down, but sometimes it's just fucking great to sit back and watch.

The production manager was a bastard plain and simple and he loved cutting corners and costs just as much as the muckety mucks further up the chain. He was forever tinkering with the shows budget, and it wasn't uncommon for his little tinkers to eliminate several production assistants a day. It wasn't accidental. He always thought we had way too many on staff because he'd see them sitting around during the day.

What he didn't seem to grasp was that they all had their own unique jobs they were assigned to do, and if three of them disappeared that meant three jobs were no longer assigned, which meant three more guys were about to get their workload doubled. It's fairly simple mathematics.

The Rumble in the Jungle took place in the production office in the hotel where we were staying and where the final round of judging would take place.

The producer needed more production assistants, as he did in most cities, but the production manager kept telling him there just wasn't the budget for them, which, frankly was bullshit. You cannot run any type of production without production assistants. They are the glue that keeps everything together. They are the blood pumping through the body keeping it mobile. They are the heart and soul of the show. They're whatever other similes I can come up with that make it obvious that without them the show won't go on. They do everything from the laundry, running errands and picking up the contestants to packing and unpacking. Everything little thing they do isn't magic, but it might as well be. Everything that needs to be done eventually gets delegated into the lap of a production assistant. So, it's pretty obvious, I hope, that when you don't have enough things slowly grind to a halt, stop being done properly and generally life becomes a lot less cheerful.

I was sitting across from the production manager when all hell broke loose.

The producer stormed into the room and erupted. I mean went ballistic. I didn't have a clue what the fuck was happening, but I was damned sure I didn't want to take a hit for the production manager's team, so I got the fuck out of Dodge and settled in to watch from the hallway.

The fight itself was so loud that people were drawn to it from all directions. And not just show staff, guests and hotel staff that had been in the lobby hustled up the stairs to see what the ruckus was.

The production manager was puce, and for once really didn't have a lot to say. His mouth was moving but no words were coming out. The producer stood toe-to-toe with him and ripped into him.

For once it felt like someone further up the totem pole got it, and not only got it, but was going to bat for us, and I fucking loved it. There wasn't one of us who hadn't wanted to unleash our own version of Hiroshima on the idiot, but without kissing goodbye to simple necessities like rent money and food, we couldn't.

I had the biggest shit-eating grin on my face. I don't even remember how long the fight lasted, but there was only one winner, a straight knock-out in the third with production manager flat out on the canvas and little blue canaries tweeting as they flew in circles around his head. And he didn't need a single punch to put the guy down.

DID SHE OR DIDN'T SHE?

Randy was the only one who actually knew my name and made an effort to say "Hello" to me each time he saw me. Simon didn't. Paula didn't know her own name for most of the time. Ryan didn't. I always found that interesting, in a good way. We probably interacted the least of the lot, but he took the time to know who was who around him.

The production manager's sister-in-law ended up on the road with us as an assistant. She claimed that she was paying for her own way the entire time, but the more we flew and the more hotels we stayed in the more she would have had to have been related to the Rockefeller's to keep us believing she was paying her travel expenses. They amounted to quite a bit more than she was making each week.

She was in charge of the judge's room and overseeing the judges and their assistants during the tour. Her job was essentially the same during the final round in every city: just be there in case they need anything, help out the other production assistants, coordinate the breakdown of the room when the judging was all over, but mainly focus on the judges and keeping them happy.

She would take their lunch orders and then pass them on to me, and then I would pass them on to our contact at the venue, who would have the kitchen staff whip up whatever they wanted.

There was talk.

There's always talk in an environment like this, but this talk was more explicit, less behind-the-back-of-the-hand talk, and it was backed up by the evidence of everybody's eyes.

The talk was that she had her eye on one of the judges.

As I said, there was a lot of eyewitness evidence to support the talk. They weren't shy about flirting with each other even though the room was crowded with other employees. She had a fairly standard uniform of T-shirt, jeans, and running shoes. She wore the same stuff every day save for the last day in Greensboro, where she turned up in high heels, a low cut top that showed her plastic tits off nicely, and a short, short skirt.

There aren't many days on the audition tour where fuck-me pumps are the way to go, and certainly not the last day in an audition stop.

But, of course, her brother-in-law had left for Las Vegas (leaving me in charge) and with the cat away it was hardly surprising the mouse wanted to play.

At the end of the day she brought the box of shot tapes to the production office and tossed them on the table before turning on her heel and walking out. Everyone figured that she would be off doing what she had to do before the tear down, packing up the judging room so we in turn could pack the eighteen wheeler and send the driver on his way to the next city.

Thirty minutes or so later a call came over the walkie-talkie asking what they should do with the judging room.

By now it ought to have been done and ready to load.

The fact that nothing had been done yet was ridiculous. It was throwing everything off schedule. The guy in charge of the production assistants started helping them break things down and I went back to the production office to try to get her on the phone and figure out what was going on. I called her cellphone. No answer. I called it again. No answer. And again and again. I had the front desk at the hotel call her room. Nada. I left message after message. Not a peep.

Several hours later she finally deigned to reply.

And of course she had a ready excuse. Apparently she was upset by the attitude of the production office when she turned in the tapes. If it smells like a turd, my friends, if it smells like a turd...

The first thing everyone thought was that she had wound up back at the hotel with said judge. After all, why else bail at the same time the judges were leaving the venue, and more to the point, why else would she be dressed like a low-class hooker?

Unlike our beloved ex-President, she neither confirmed nor denied anything.

And us folks with nothing better to do, we were left pondering one of the unsolved mysteries of the Season 5 audition tour.

Did she or didn't she?

ROLLING THE DICE WITH AN 18-WHEELER

If you think the hours that we worked were unbelievable, you can't begin to imagine what it was like for the truck driver who was hired to haul all the equipment across the Great Wide Open. The road schedule was every bit as insane and overly optimistic as everything else on the show, and didn't allow for the guy to have any downtime between hauls meaning he was up for anywhere from twenty four to forty eight hours at a time, driving.

There's nothing good about a driver having to go two entire days on the road without the luxury of a rest stop nap. He explained to me how on the worst of the hauls he'd have to piss in a bottle while he drove and pour it out the window because he couldn't afford to lose any time. So what they say about no matter how bad you've got it, someone out there has it worse, he was that someone.

The guy was great.

I loved shooting the shit with him. There was something about him, a genuine quality that reminded me of someone that I'd find in my hometown. And despite everything, he stayed happy and loved sharing tall stories. I don't think many – if any – of them were true but that didn't make a blind bit of difference. Sometimes it's just as great to listen to the staggering stories of Baron Munchausen as it is to the wisdom of Uncle Remus.

But I don't for one minute think the guy knew what he was signing up for when he agreed to be the driver for the show. It would take a special kind of lunatic to willingly volunteer knowing everything, but truckers are a special breed of guy, so who knows? After a while our only so called 'time off' was when we were in the air flying to the next city. We arrived, we headed straight to the venue and he was expected to be there already, waiting for us so we could get straight to unloading everything. I'm not sure where the hell his 'time off' was hidden.

One of the things I disliked most about the entire Idol set up, as you've probably noticed if you've been reading between the lines, was the utter lack of concern toward staff welfare. We were putting in 15 hours a day, seven days a week, the truck driver was pulling forty-eight hour shifts. It was as though we became a commodity that could be gambled with, like a set of chips at the roulette table. It had been made damn clear to everyone that we were replaceable. It felt as though the guys at the top of the totem pole ran the numbers, worked out what were and weren't acceptable losses and rolled the dice with our lives. And by numbers I mean the human cost, the fiscal cost and the time costs of this punishing schedule and decided that the gains from time and finance outweighed the potential human costs.

Someone somewhere had to have thought about it, had to have made a conscious decision that a seven day rolling schedule was X amount more efficient than an eight day rolling schedule and to hell with the guys who have to live by it. Factor in a certain amount of natural attrition, the lazy dropping off along the road, factor in local help powering through seven days (meaning no need to fear the same burnout that someone working the four month tour would) and you start to get a proper view of the Idol equation. And, remember, no matter how stacked the costs are, they're never going to tip the scales away from the Almighty Dollar on the other side of the balance.

So it was viable to put the truck driver's life in jeopardy by scheduling forty-eight hour hauls, and as far as the economics were concerned that meant it must have been a viable 'expense' to endanger all of those other drivers sharing the road with him.

NOW I KNOW HE WAS JUST DOING HIS JOB THE SAME WAY WE ALL WERE.

American Idol made some sort of conscious or unconscious calculation and decided their demands were important enough to make putting his life and all of those other driver's lives at risk worthwhile. It was no different to how my life was used as the ball in the roulette wheel when I was driving the fifteen passenger van in Boston. Red or black? Odd or even? How's your luck?

He'd roll into town on time – never late, never early – completely exhausted. Exhausted to the point that he would sleep in the cab for the next two to three days, only emerging from the nest he'd made up there to take a leak in the restroom or grab a bite to eat.

We can all talk about being pushed to the limits of endurance and tolerance, but I think he genuinely was skating along a very dangerous precipice. I mean, it ain't easy to stay awake for forty-eight hours when you're at home, but to be stuck behind the wheel of a long haul truck battling against sleep? That's just plain scary and a little bit stupid.

When trucks crash they crash. It's never a bump in the road, it's a turn, a jack knife, a tumble, fireball crash and too many times people don't walk away from them.

So why load the dice and make the gamble more difficult?
I don't get it.
Surely a day here, a day there isn't worth that sort of cost?

A RANDOM ACT OF KINDNESS

Las Vegas was more chaotic than it had been during the other tours. Things were happening in the real world that impacted on the schedules and plans and no amount of "But we are with *American Idol*." was ever going to take precedence over the relief efforts of Hurricane Katrina, for instance. We had to fly the Austin shortlist out to Vegas and add them to the roster there because our Austin venue was needed for evacuees.

Like most people, I tried my best to follow the news of the disaster, not the least because it was an eye-openingly massive failure by our government and no amount of sound bites or pressed flesh and media spin was going to change that. I'd had such an amazing time in New Orleans a year prior and couldn't imagine the turmoil and tragedy unfolding. It was so very sobering to see pictures of the streets that I had been walking down, and the restaurants that I had eaten at, the landmarks I had visited devastated now by the floodwaters.

It was so much more intimate and immediate than the tragedy out in South East Asia when the tsunami hit Indonesia and along the coastline. This was home, so it hit home, if that makes sense?

I couldn't make up my mind if it made what we were doing less or more important, which may sound ridiculous when you consider the loss of life, the loss of homes and possessions, of entire communities, that both of these disasters had wrought, but everything we were doing in this world of make-believe provided distraction from the suffering and sometimes, well, sometimes I don't think being distracted is all that bad, is it? It wasn't like we were out there saving lives, but we had kids out of New Orleans coming to the auditions in the wake of Katrina, just as we'd had them coming before the storm. It didn't change things.

Part of me wanted to walk out on the show and volunteer for the relief effort, as though one more pair of hands might make all of the difference.

As the contestants were shuttled from the airport to the hotel in Vegas several of the production staff lined up and greeted them and explained what was going to be taking place over the next day or two. It was all fairly standard stuff, apart from one girl, and she's burnt into my brain. She stepped off the shuttle sobbing. I've seen people crying of course, but this was different, these sobs wracked her body to the point that she couldn't stand on her own two feet. I've never been all that comfortable around crying. I feel awkward and clumsy, like whatever I am going to do or say is just going to make it worse, and I feel stupid asking someone who is obviously breaking their heart if everything's okay.

But everything in this life isn't about me. So, I approached her to see what was wrong and ask if there was anything that I could do.

It wasn't anything special in terms of loved ones washed away in the flood, or anything horrible like that. It was just simple honest to God sadness. She had never been away from her husband and children for a single night, and she couldn't afford a cellphone so couldn't call them to see how they were and tell them she was okay. Like I said, simple, normal.

We had all these stupid rules on the show about not interacting with the contestants, but for the price of a phone call and a few minutes of kindness I could make at least some of her pain go away, so why the hell shouldn't I? I gave her my cell and told her to call home. When they answered her knees buckled and she went down on her knees, tears streaming down her face. A few minutes and a random act of kindness. If only all of life's pains could be eased so simply.

FEDERAL EXPRESS THE HARD WAY

Wylleen showed up in Las Vegas to work with us for a couple days.

She would only make an appearance in other cities if things were going wrong. If things were good, she was nowhere to be seen, but if they were going tits up, it reflected badly on her so she'd wade into the middle of things with all the grace and subtlety of a ten ton elephant and make them worse.

It was invariably the same, she'd waddle into the production office and everyone would smile and kiss her ample backside.

I ignored her.

Why should I smile and buy into the wonder that was Wylleen May when all I was to her was a doormat and convenient scapegoat? Not a city went by where I wasn't the recipient of her vile temper. Not that I was special. She was an equal opportunity bitch.

I had my back to her the entire time she was in the production office. We're talking a few days here. Every morning I ignored her when she walked in to the room, and all day I did my best to ignore her.

But ignoring people is difficult when their idea of good office communication skills includes throwing a Federal Express shipping envelope (the heavy duty cardboard ones), along with the paperwork she needed sent inside it, directly at the back of my head. When the package hit the ground, she yelled, "Mail that!" and went back to whatever she was doing before. I had to bite my tongue.

Mailing it in this new mood of mine involved me kicking the package out the door and following it as it went down the stairs.

DR. PHIL

And our story has come full circle, back to the final few days in the office.

Oddly, and it may be difficult to believe having read the preceding tales of Idol madness, I can, hand-on-heart say that after all the bullshit, all the verbal and physical abuse, all of the stupidity and vindictiveness I don't really feel any anger towards her.

I'd like to say that I was a big enough man to feel sympathy for her, actually. Sympathy because she was always so very obviously miserable inside her own skin. So miserable that one of the only ways she had of validating herself, and of feeling any relief from the misery that was her life was to take her anger out on people around her. Maybe if she found someone to love she'd mutate into a decent person.

At least that's what I think Doctor Phil would say.

Me, I am not a TV shrink, and I'm not in the habit of believing six impossible things before breakfast, so let's just say I am not going to hold my breath.

THE GENE SIMMONS SHOW

Having made my mind up that I needed a new job, I started applying for production coordinator and manager positions.

After a couple weeks back in LA, I received a call from the executive in charge of production for Gene Simmons' Family Jewels asking me if I could come in for an interview. I said yes, but now I just needed to figure out how to make it happen because the new production manager was so unsure of himself that if I was gone from my desk for more than just a couple minutes he would be ringing my phone and asking why I wasn't there. It had gotten to the point where I felt like I needed to call in a hostage negotiator to sort out some fresh air for me. I needed to find a solid reason to come in late one day so I could go the job interview. I lied and said that I had an abscess that was causing me to be physically ill.

The interview went well and I went back to Idol to prep for the next round of auditions. The clock, though, was ticking.

FULL CIRCLE

Which brings us back to page one of this book.

I was offered the job on Gene Simmons Family Jewels, but couldn't simply walk away from Idol without giving my two-weeks notice.

And the circle is complete...

EASILY REPLACED?

But the story isn't over.

Not by a long way.

I stayed in touch with a few people, the office slut for one, because she kept me entertained with her sordid stories of sex, drugs, and rock and roll. She was very proud of the fact that she had nailed one of the contestants from Season 5 (one the male standouts who has gone on to have an serious singing career unlike the winner, Taylor Hicks, that should help you work out who). She volunteered to stay at the apartments and watch over the contestants with intentions of turning six and nine into sixty-nine whenever she could.

Remember that Fox exec she'd snared on the road? Stupid fool fell in love with her after all of their sordid little liaisons, left his wife for her, only for the studio slut to walk away. Sometimes it isn't all *Pretty Woman* in Tinsel Town.

In those last couple of weeks, right around Hollywood Week, they hired another guy to act as the senior production coordinator. He'd be my direct boss for my last few weeks, or he would have been if he hadn't hurt is back on the job after a couple of days. He was in so much pain that he couldn't do anything without experiencing crippling pain and when it wasn't getting better he decided to go to the doctor, who advised him to stay in bed for a couple of weeks to rest his back.

Obviously that went down like a lead balloon with Wylleen who gave him her classic ultimatum: come into to work or find a new job. He quit.

And then there was the girl that was hired to take over my position. She didn't last very long either. She worked through maybe two weeks of Wylleen's crap and then she walked away in the middle of afternoon. Like most production employees she'd been promised that she'd only be working so many hours, and all of those other promises they'd made me when I was originally hired. She didn't buy into their lies, and good for her.

I wish I had been half as smart.

HOLLYWOOD GOSSIP INSIDER? WHO ME?

Then there was the *big* revelation.

I found out that I hadn't actually been paid properly during my time with *American Idol*. We're not talking a few bucks here or there, either. I was owed a lot of money in back pay and overtime pay.

I'd grown up reading gossip mags and tabloids and knew they always quoted their insider sources, and thought that selling some of my stories to these tabloids might help recoup some of the missing money.

I still had several friends on the show who I chatted with over Instant Messenger and phoned every once in a while, so I decided to see if I could get any 'behind the scenes' dirt on anyone who was a part of the show. It didn't take long before three of my former co-workers were spilling all the dirt about who was doing what to whom while the cameras were off. Each week I would make notes about my conversations with my former co-workers and pitch them around to the tabloids. Whoever offered the highest dollar and cent amount got the stories and I became one of those Hollywood Gossip Insiders I'd loved reading when I'd been growing up, completing another circle of my journey.

What surprised me was how easy it was to wheedle the

gossip out of the staff, and once wheedled, just how easy it was to sell this stuff.

THE IDOL TRUTH TOUR

As the world turns, my employment with Gene Simmons Family Jewels ran its course and within a few days of finishing I was contacted by a former Idol employee (who also had issues with the show including the strong arm techniques and threats that eventually caused her to quit the show) to tell me about a campaign that the Writers Guild of America West was involved in against FremantleMedia, *American Idol,* and other shows that essentially scammed money from their employees by not paying overtime and/or not allowing employees proper, State of California required, meal and rest breaks.

It was another eye-opening conversation. Obviously I knew full well I ticked all of the boxes when it came to having been taken advantage of, not paid overtime, and not given any proper meal breaks or rest periods, so as soon as I hung up with her I got on the phone with the Writers Guild. Better to get the proper information, straight from the horse's mouth, so to speak, rather than get worked up over more gossip.

We made arrangements and I went in for a face-to-face meeting to get the rundown on what was going.

The Writers Guild were accusing production companies of not paying their employees properly and withholding money, while at the same time violating California labor laws. I feel like I've been banging a big bass drum when it comes to the unbelievable hours Idol demanded of us, sometimes in excess of eighty or ninety hours a week, turning in seven days a week as was typical for the Season 5 audition tour. I've already gone into a little detail about what happened when I tried to turn in my actual hours on my time cards, and how each time I tried they were returned to me saying that I needed to deliver a generic time card with twelve hours written, with a one hour break, and that each day needed to look identical hour wise.

I am sure there were times that people were paid overtime, but from what I recall they were about as rare as pink fluffy bunnies and unicorns.

I worked with the Writers Guild trying to figure out how much in overtime and meal and rest period penalties I was owed. There was a limitation period to the claim so anything that I was going to include in my wage claim case had to fall within the limitation period. I didn't have anything to lose by filing a wage claim case against the show.

I wasn't alone.

Several other former Idol employees filed claims.

It was peanuts when we worked it out – I just hadn't realized quite how many peanuts. We worked out a rough total from my first to last day of employment stood at roughly $300,000.

Yep, you read that right, five zeros, comma in the right place, three at the front. $300,000. Like I said, a lot of peanuts.

But run the numbers in your head, how many days I was there, the fact that I was never given an hour lunch break, despite being forced to lie by the show for payroll purposes, I claimed for each and every day during my employment. The rest of the money calculated was based on overtime pay that had been worked but shaved off the time cards. In other words overtime that I had been cheated out of.

There's a rule about filing these wage claim cases (it was explained to me by the Writers Guild West legal team) that means that if you have a management title on the show and it's reflected on your pay stubs and time cards then you cannot file a claim. The reasoning is that it is understood and within reason that managers need to be on call around the clock because that's part of their job. The other important rule is that you can't have the power to hire and fire any employees. I was only the production coordinator on the show, and thus had no management responsibilities (taking all of my direction from the production manager and Wylleen herself who also did the hiring and firing).

Upon filing the various cases the Writers Guild West asked me if I would be the face of their campaign.

I agreed, knowing that I would finally be able to speak out against *American Idol* and how they exploited their employees. It was around this time that I met Aaron Bale in the Roosevelt Hotel, which of course is where this book started, when he agreed to help me put my thoughts in words and help me truly be heard, and for that and his help I'll be forever grateful. I'd made a point of trying to stand up for myself while on the show, I'd fought to be paid the money I was rightfully owed, but the harder I fought the harder I hit the brick wall of: 'if I wanted to stay in my job I needed to shut the fuck up and just do that job.' The first rule of the Idol Club is you do not mention the Payroll. But now, with the help of the Writers Guild West (and later with Aaron's help) I would finally have my outlet to tell the real truth about how employees were treated.

Step one was a press conference. It was set up outside the labor office in Van Nuys, California, and I was the key speaker at the event.

I had never really spoken in public before, not since school, not in front of dozens of cameras and radio station mics, but this was my time, this was my chance, and I had no idea if I would ever get it again, so swallowed the nerves and ran with it.

Finally being able to speak out was liberating.

And after the press conference I was asked to take part in several rallies and protests against the show. The Writers Guild West had plans to follow Idol around the country while they held the auditions for the next season. Again I agreed to be a part of it. I spoke at a press conference in Los Angeles before boarding a bus with dozens of other Writers Guild West members and supporters as we embarked for a protest rally outside of the Cow Palace. I spoke at another press conference in San Francisco and meet with several city officials. Over the Idol Truth tour I gave dozens of interviews, telling my story to everyone who wanted to hear it.

We traveled on to New York City and held a huge peaceful protest, effectively shutting down the entire Manhattan block where FremantleMedia had its offices. They knew we were coming, they knew exactly what it was about and what was going to happen, and instead of standing up for themselves and being counted, making a statement, defending their actions, they turned their office lights off and shut the blinds.

A damning indictment if ever there was one.

THE OUTCOME WAS ALREADY DECIDED

I wasn't Don Quixotic going into this tilting at windmills. I knew there was a possibility I could emerge victorious, but I wasn't naïve enough to think winning was ever really likely. Thankfully it wasn't about winning, it had stopped being about that, and it wasn't about the money, it had never been about that. It was about fighting. When everything was boiled down to its fundamental core, the most important thing to me was that I actually stood up and let myself be counted. And not just for me, Justin Buckles, but for all of the production assistants and coordinators and gaffers and riggers and truckers and every other 'little guy' in the entertainment industry who had been treated like shit, worked into the ground, abused, lied to, and it became every bit as noble and every bit as helpless as Cervantes' hero's cause.

Certainly it was important to me to be the face of the Writers Guild West campaign, and it was important to me to tell the truth. I can't force people to believe me, I can't force them to accept everything out of my mouth as gospel, but again, that's not half as important as simply giving them the information, letting them process it and come to their own conclusions about what went on behind the scenes, and to evaluate for themselves the high cost of this so-called reality television. I've done a lot of stuff I am not proud of, but this was something worthy of pride.

So it came to the day of the claim hearing. All of the wage claim cases are recorded so the person overseeing the case can replay what has been discussed to help them make their final decision. One of the first things he said, and I swear it was before he started recording the session, was along the lines of, "I really don't want to see any more cases like this, so I don't want you to file any more of them, and I don't want you to encourage any of your friends to file any in the future."

I knew right then and there that he had already made up his mind to rule against me.

I could understand his decision. Remember the labor division knew that this problem was rampant in the entertainment industry. If he ruled in my favor, he'd set a precedent, and of course you could bet I'd be very vocal about, which would only encourage hundreds, if not thousands of similar cases to be filed, crippling the labor division and costing millions.

So I had to content myself with the fact that I had had the opportunity to speak out against the show and the corruption that goes on behind the scenes.

AND THE MORAL OF THE STORY?

A parting word... a moral to this story, if you will.

At times I was a jerk, at times I was a hypocrite, at times I was weak. I was all of these things and more because I'm a normal guy, I'm not the hero of some Hollywood movie. I didn't scoop the studio slut up in my arms (dressed in white naval uniform) and walk out to an orchestral fanfare of Joe Cocker's *Up Where We Belong*. But then, she wasn't Debra Winger and me, I'm no Richard Gere.

Equally I won't try to tell you it was a living hell. It was hard. Sure it was. It was exhausting. Dispiriting and all of that, but it was also a blast. I have accumulated some fantastic memories, and even a few decent stories. I have sucked the marrow out of life, and I'm damned proud of what I accomplished, moving from a small town in Oregon to Los Angeles and working on the number one show in America.

I'll always be proud of that, and with good reason.

But I will always be angry with myself for allowing myself to be taken advantage of like that. I will always be disappointed with myself because I fell for the lies, because I didn't stand up and because, ultimately, I enabled Wylleen's abuse. I'll forever be furious with myself for allowing the executives to brainwash me into thinking that they would blacklist me and my fear made me miss precious days and weeks with my father at the end, time that I could never get back and should never have given up.

All of these things and more, they're all still swirling around inside me. There are hundreds of small and not so small ways my time with Idol has affected me, and some of those affects have been profound – to the point that finally, sitting here today writing these last few words, I finally realize who I am.

I'm the Lucky Buck...

You'd forgotten about that dollar bill I claimed from the bulletin board on my last day, hadn't you?

Where'd you think I got my nickname?

www.ingramcontent.com/pod-product-compliance
Lightning Source LLC
Chambersburg PA
CBHW032059090426
42743CB00007B/175